Bachelors of Citizenship

A Sequel to Step Forward America!-
A Case for a National Service
Program

Ted Hollander

BACHELORS OF CITIZENSHIP
A Sequel to Step Foward America!-
A Case for a National Service Program

Craigston Books
Sherman, CT 06784
860-354-6423

ISBN 978-0-578-33146-1

Manufactured in the United States of America
First printing February 2021
Second edition May 2021
Third edition October 2021

To my children and grandchildren who are already walking the path to good citizenship. May we continue to pave the way for them and future generations.

Table of Contents

Introduction

There is nothing wrong with America that cannot be cured by what is right with America.

William Jefferson Clinton

Most of us agree that closing the social and economic gap between the working class and the more privileged is one of the major challenges of our great nation and that it begins with education.

Endless deliberations take place in Washington concerning every domestic or foreign policy issue bill being considered in Congress, and it's quite obvious that ideology is trumping the good of the nation. Both sides of the aisle are so afraid of antagonizing their constituencies and losing votes in future elections that they have become completely impotent.

This need for a better educated and informed electorate has wide support by liberals, conservatives and virtually all others who do not fit any particular label. An informed electorate would not permit their elected officials to get away with session after session of inaction. An informed electorate would, if necessary, override the dictates of those who insist on imposing for the 21st century the strictest interpretation of a constitution designed for the 18th century; and an informed electorate would demand of its leaders new amendments capable of ensuring that our government remains functional.

Unfortunately, many of us see the education issue as simply a matter of providing for all a college education or path to a college education or perhaps in some cases a fallback of a trade school or apprenticeship for those not suited to or desirous of a college education. I contend and will show you that there is a third, and for many, a much better way of uplifting them, especially those in the working class.

For most of us after completing high school, four years of college culminating in a degree in the arts or sciences has always been considered the ultimate education of an enlightened citizen, whether or not any training specific to a particular occupation is included. And I have always supported this thinking. Now, however, as I advocate for my "lessons in living," I think we should reconsider. While still firmly believing in the value of the courses taught in the humanities, arts and sciences, I no longer think it necessary to include them in a four year period between secondary education and employment unless the courses studied relate specifically to an occupation being pursued, for example medicine, law, business, computer technology, or to any career in the arts and humanities being pursued. If the courses studied are merely to foster an appreciation for the fine performing and visual arts that contribute to our quality of life, or an understanding of the basics of the physical laws that govern the universe and our place in it, then there are a multitude of opportunities to learn them later on in life. There is continuing adult education via online courses, and an abundance of educational offerings by museums and other organizations devoted to the arts, the sciences and our history.

We have also been led to believe that a college education teaches us to think creatively for ourselves and also to appreciate the thoughts and opinions of others with whom we differ. Some college courses may accomplish this, but many others would not. I would say that it's more likely that if one isn't already taught to think creatively and objectively by the time they complete high school, one cannot really be prepared to even embark on a college education.

I offer a core curriculum that can be taught in primary and secondary education, and reinforced in the basic training phase of a national service program that will indeed teach us to think creatively and objectively, and will be the foundation for elevating low and middle skilled low paying jobs in order to provide a suitable standard of living, for the pursuit of happiness, and most importantly for becoming an enlightened, engaged and productive "good citizen." And these subjects can also be further explored in post-secondary education.

And it is vital that these lessons be learned before exercising the right to vote, and before striking out on one's own in the work a day world and/or starting and raising a family—in short, as you will see, before it's too late.

Let me assure you that while the subject of this tome might frighten one into thinking that it will be loaded with dry statistics, that is not the case, as you will shortly ascertain. I merely am trying to present a "big idea" or concept, if you will, that hopefully will get enough people thinking that it's a good idea so that the pundits, the social scientists, and educators—categories for none of which I qualify—will run with the ball and determine what aspects can be implemented and to what extent. As I say, think in terms of a "big idea."

Follow me on the path to becoming a good citizen and even earning a degree in citizenship.

Chapter One
Make/Keep America Great...First...Exceptional

> *These unhappy times call for the building of plans that...build from the bottom up and not from the top down, that put their faith once more in the forgotten man at the bottom of the economic pyramid.*
>
> *Franklin Delano Roosevelt*
> *radio address, April 7, 1932*

Regardless of our ideology or party affiliation, if there is one overarching feature that we can take away from the previous Trump administration, it is the issue of what makes or keeps us, America, great or exceptional. We are subjected to a constant stream of new books, articles, news reports, and social media postings addressing this. And this is a "good thing." A stated position on this can serve as a good background or starting point when advocating social or economic programs.

First in Global Leadership
I am on record in previous writings that making "America First" or "America Great" again or still, cannot be done by merely protecting America's selfinterests as President Donald Trump saw it, but, more in line with

President Biden's vision, by making America First in global leadership by:

- Championing freedom at home and abroad
- Welcoming the economically and politically oppressed to make a new home here in America, and in the process, adding their own contributions to the nation's rich diversity
- Advancing the war against poverty
- Saving and protecting the planet and its resources for the use and enjoyment of all
- Defeating radical Islamic Jihad and other terrorist movements
- Protecting the rights of all to trade and travel freely on the high seas

If we can do this, we will be in a commanding position to eventually achieve lasting peace by negotiating non-aggression treaties between us and our European allies with Russia, and between us and our Pacific allies with China, and nuclear arms reduction treaties with all the nuclear states and agreements with the major polluters to combat climate change. Then perhaps we can all benefit from a United Nations that acts as a mediator for all of us after we have committed to these paths toward peace.

A Better Educated and Informed Electorate

But I also believe that we can't make America great, again or still, without a universal commitment to a social program at home that includes a national service program and a new focus on certain aspects of our education system that combined will address what I see as the five major threats to our democracy, to our way of life, in fact to our very survival. These are the root causes of our inability to govern, take action and make progress

- First, too many of us no longer trust our governing and justice institutions
- Second, many of us have substituted the social media for the opinions of experts as our source of news
- Third, we are divided by the extreme positions of our two political parties and are no longer able to compromise. Obstruction has taken the place of governing
- Fourth, concern for community has been replaced by our concern for self—as our concern for our global neighbors and for the globe itself has deteriorated.
- And finally, all of this exacerbates our unwillingness and/or inability to properly address the threat of global warming as addressed in the latest UN report, as well as other threats, internal like pandemics, or external like the actions of rogue or authoritarian states.

With rare exception, we no longer function as the founders intended.

So, here is what I propose: inclusion in our primary and secondary education new or expanded courses in civics, media literacy and other subjects fostering good citizenship that I call "lessons in living, a common core for a citizen corps", followed by a one or two year civilian or military service term for all 18 year old men and women. The term would start with a mandatory three-month training camp that includes not only basic military training but also an educational component reinforcing the above "lessons in living." The remainder of the term would be voluntary serving here or abroad in one of the existing service programs, e.g., AmeriCorps, a yet to be developed service organization, or one of our USAID programs.

This will address the five threats I describe by:

First, and this is arguably the most critical and important aspect of a universal national service program, <u>living, learning and working together</u> with others from diverse backgrounds, all youth will become more aware of our social, economic and political challenges, will understand conflicting views on the issues, will become productive involved citizens to take action to confront the issues, will vote and hold our elected officials accountable to negotiate, compromise and govern rather than obstruct, and will be better equipped and motivated to go on to higher education, the trades or other careers.

Second, we will provide our most vulnerable youth with an alternate to substance abuse and trafficking, gang membership, gun violence, radicalization by foreign or domestic terrorist groups, and other antisocial behavior.

Third, we will all, our children and ourselves, have some skin in the game. With our rights as outlined in the Constitution and our other privileges come responsibilities. For these rights and privileges, we should do more than just pay our taxes.

We should not leave the heavy lifting of defending our country, or of supporting our democracy in other ways, to the small minority of individuals who currently serve in the military or in one of our present voluntary service organizations. We should all have a voice in, and accept responsibility for, our political and military actions.

Fourth, we will build a massive partially trained military and civilian service resource to respond to natural disasters and multiple other threats, both domestic and foreign, to our security.

Fifth, We will massively increase manpower devoted to serving the needy, the elderly and infirmed, and the homeless, in social services, schools and healthcare in low income communities, assisting in border patrol and immigration processing, increasing inspections at ports to find drugs and other contraband, and performing forestry practices, for example fire break clearing, to combat wildfires.

Sixth, We will head our youth in the direction of public service better equipped to be part of a much needed and much larger diplomatic corps that will encourage other countries to join us in combatting not only climate change but the ever growing threats of a nuclear conflict with North Korea or China, and other challenges that can no longer he effectively addressed militarily. <u>Our military might has its limits as was so clearly demonstrated in Afghanistan.</u>

And finally, we will rebuild our national pride and international respect by replacing some of our international economic aid that gets siphoned off by corrupt governments with in person humanitarian aid provided by the Peace Corps and our international development programs.

Let's not give up and succumb to the economic pressure of China, or step aside and let Vladimir Putin or the criminal regimes of North Korea and Iran push us around.

And it is the first of the above goals that I wish to explore now. With a government that will guarantee that we all have an equal opportunity for employment leading to a standard of living that gives us adequate food, shelter, healthcare and education, and that truly encourages our pursuit of happiness, we can indeed be the great America that cares not only for its citizens, but for all the inhabitants of the planet and for the planet itself.

The issue is a new look at how we expose ourselves to diverse ideas and educate ourselves accordingly, not a replacement for our current thinking, but more like a rearranging of some of it.

I had contended that all of America's ills could be cured by a universal national service program, when in 2015 I published the first edition of *Step Forward America!—A Case for a National Service Program*. That surely was, and is still, a big, big idea!

But then, why don't we have a truly universal national service program? We are a nation of individuals who cherish our independence above all else. We take pride in our hard work to get ahead. We are considered a nation of volunteers, but we don't like anyone, especially the government telling us what to do.

Let's take a brief look at the earlier history of our volunteer service efforts. Prior to 9-11 (September 11, 2001), these included:

> 1910 American philosopher William James in his book *The Moral Equivalent of War* envisioned conscription of the whole youthful population to balance the injustice of wars and for the good of the commonwealth.

> 1933-1942 in the aftermath of the depression millions of young people served from 6 to 18 paid months in Franklin Roosevelt's Civilian Conservation Corps restoring national parks, fighting forest fires, and maintaining wildlife habitats, and supporting their families.

> 1944 The Servicemen's Readjustment Act known as the GI Bill offered education opportunities in return for their service during the war.

1960s National Senior Service Corps commonly known as Senior Corps was established to help seniors find opportunities for service in their communities.

1961 John Kennedy established the Peace Corps.

1964 Lyndon Johnson created VISTA, Volunteers in Service to America, now part of AmeriCorps, providing opportunities for volunteers to help in low-income communities.

1989-1990 President George H. W. Bush creates the National Community Service Act authorizing grants for in school service learning and other youth service opportunities, and the Points of Light Foundation to encourage volunteering.

1990 William F. Buckley publishes *Gratitude* describing a comprehensive compelling proposal for 18 year old's to serve 1 year of voluntary civilian service

1993 President Clinton created AmeriCorps and the Corporation for National and Community Service. By the time he left office 200,000 had served, more than in the entire 40 years of Peace Corps

Then, after 9-11 there was understandably a new focus on national service.

President Bush created USA Freedom Corps to promote more service opportunities, Citizen Corps to meet homeland defense needs, and Volunteers for Prosperity mobilizing teachers, doctors and technical professionals. He requested increased funding for Peace Corps, AmeriCorps and Senior Corps, and in 2002 asked all Americans to devote 2 years of their life to national service.

By the end of his 2nd term 61 million Americans had answered the call in one fashion or another.

2003 the Brookings Institution publishes *United We Serve,* a compilation of essays and opinion pieces on national service and the future of citizenship

2004 AmeriCorps funding was increased to cover 75,000 participants.

2009 President Obama signs the Edward M. Kennedy Serve America Act sponsoring 2 million volunteers in AmeriCorps, Senior Corps and additional student and community programs.

2012 The Aspen Institute implemented the Franklin Project which morphed into the Service Year Alliance headed up by General Stanley McChrystal with the goal of making universal national service a reality. The campaign Serve America Together and current Service Year pilot program continue this effort.

Over the next decade there was considerable comment by elected officials, journalists and others recommending national service. And in the 2020 Democratic primaries many of the candidates came out strongly in favor of a universal program, a national commission having done likewise earlier in the year.

Well, while I surely did not trigger the response, in March 2020 the National Commission on Military, National and Public Service concluding a three-year study published and presented to the President, Congress and the people, their Final Report, *Inspired to Serve,* strongly recommending a universal service program. And we now have a bill in the Senate promoting a promising step in this direction, the Cultivating Opportunity and Response to the Pandemic through Service (CORPS) Act recommending significant additional funding for AmeriCorps Vista, the Peace Corps, Senior Corps and like organizations. The bill is sponsored by Sen. Chris Coons of Delaware and a bipartisan group of colleagues. While this bill is promoted as a response to the COVID-19 pandemic, we hope that this funding level will continue as the pandemic fades. Increased funding for these organizations is one of the significant recommendations in the Final Report from the National Commission on Military, National and Public Service. A similar bill, the Promoting National Service and Reducing Unemployment Act had also been introduced in the House of Representatives.

Florida Governor Ron DeSantis also picked up on this and proposes to use $106 million of his states coronavirus stimulus funds to support civics education.

Now, however, included in President Biden's $3.5 trillion Build Back Better budget is The Civilian Climate

Corps for Jobs and Justice Act earmarking $30 billion to fund 1 1/2 million young Americans in projects that help communities respond to climate change and transition to a clean economy. This is patterned after FDR's Civilian Conservation Corps and, if enacted, would represent a major step forward in the direction of universal national service.

The basic concept is, of course, to get everyone off the bench and into the game in order to better prepare us to govern ourselves truly "by the people," as the founders envisioned. But, I included in my proposal one critical caveat, and that was that those coming off the bench would be educated and enlightened in a fashion that would ensure that they would be good citizens and indeed socially, economically and intellectually capable of playing the game. And that is what this book is all about—an educational component that, when added to a universal national service program, forms a second key pillar supporting good citizenship.

The national program that I envisioned was mandatory for all reaching the age of eighteen and/or having graduated from high school, and it had both a military and civilian service option. This would be an ideal setting to ensure, in addition to the obvious benefits to the nation of a huge corps of military, national and public servants, many character building benefits—exposure to living and working together with others of diverse backgrounds and opinions, and a time and place for a very comprehensive educational experience in what I call "lessons in living"—those subjects that really teach us to live in today's environment but that are not taught, or not taught adequately, in the arts and sciences curricula of traditional secondary and higher education. It is critical that these lessons be learned early in life before striking out on one's own.

Finally, after talking about it off and on for decades since World War II, a universal national service program of some sort will quite likely become a reality. However, unfortunately, at least in my thinking, the program being considered, as outlined in the above report, will be voluntary, not mandatory. Therefore, possibly with the exception of those opting for the military experience, and perhaps a limited number of those who go into civilian service in special assignments that require a large number of participants working and living together, this opportunity for exposure to others of diverse backgrounds and opinions, and an opportunity to absorb the above lessons in living will not be there. And so, we will have to provide other opportunities throughout the primary, secondary and higher education pathway for these, and tailor the national service program to include a mandatory basic training period in order to provide for the benefits of living, learning and working together with others of diverse backgrounds. From here on, I will refer to the above mentioned lessons in living simply as "lessons," "these lessons" or "our lessons."

Much is being written these days about the fall of American leadership, the end of the "American Dream," the inaction of our government, the failure of our institutions, the question of American racism, and the potential solutions to all of them. I will attempt to identify the challenges in simplest terms. We all agree that we are increasingly being divided into classes defined by our wealth, or lack of same, and the resultant availability of the basics of a standard of living that affords us adequate food, shelter, education and healthcare, with enough left over for the "pursuit of happiness."

I will touch on many areas on which we disagree and on which, after you read the book, we still will disagree. But I hope to convince you of the fundamental issue of education that must be resolved, to convince you that this is not as impossible as current thinking might have us believe, and, finally, to also convince you that the path to this resolution will also help lead us to finally achieve the dream of American exceptionalism that our forefathers envisioned. And as Puritan leader and future Governor of the Massachusetts Bay Colony, John Winthrop, yearned for in 1630, we can be that "city upon a hill" proud that "the eyes of all people are upon us."

Chapter Two
Education Objectives

> *I know no safe depository of the ulti-mate powers of the society but the peo-ple themselves; and if we think them not enlightened enough to exercise their control with a wholesome discre-tion, the remedy is not to take it from them, but to inform their discretion by education.*
>
> *Thomas Jefferson, letter to*
> *William Charles Jarvis,*
> *September 28, 1820*

We must educate with two objectives—to give every-one the opportunity to achieve for them and their family a suitable standard of living—and to sufficiently enlight-en them to become good citizens, to truly participate in "government by the people" and to hold their elected officials at all levels accountable for their decisions and actions. And this can be done without a four-year de-gree for everyone. We can educate ourselves to be good citizens more effectively and at far less cost.

I believe that the following education in the lessons in living curriculum that I will describe, preferably with a preceding, concurrent or following term of national ser-vice, is a key to the quality of life and reducing finan-cial inequality. And, if the lessons are learned early on, before one pays for four years of college, begins to earn a living, invests time and/or money in a venture, pursues a passion, or starts a family, many of the pitfalls of excess debt, misguided behavior, wasted years, and poor self-esteem can be avoided.

Three Aspects of the Funding Required to Repair Our Education System

When one considers any major change in education and lays out a detailed plan for same, "funding" becomes the immediate concern. How are we going to pay for all that is laid out in the plan? Therefore, let me start with the basics of the funding, so this concern won't be hovering over you as I outline the plan. This may seem to be putting the cart before the horse—regardless, let's get it out of the way for now. And bear in mind that most, if not all, of the funding that I advocate will be required for our education system to survive regardless of the changes that I propose.

While remodeling education is key and has its own costs, it will still take the efforts of the government via legislation to ensure access to and opportunity for the required education program that I espouse. By this I do not mean a huge continuing budget item to cover college tuition for all, although I do recommend means tested two year college tuition assistance. You will see, as you read further, I am addressing three budgetary issues, all relatively painless to correct.

Realizing the unconscionable fact that many schools in low-income areas, primarily inner city, are inadequately funded to ensure a qualified teaching staff, qualified support staff, adequate supplies, and a clean well-maintained facility, funding must be made available to correct this. This is not an option. Without this, America has no claim to being great, still or again, or to being exceptional. With the possible exception of global warming, this is the most urgent challenge facing us. Without opportunity for an equal education, there never will be opportunities for equality in housing, healthcare and pursuit of life-enriching experiences. Before we spend another nickel on an F35 fighter, we must make funding available for equal quality education for all. Without this, eventually, no matter how many F35s we have, we really won't have a nation worth fighting for.

If local taxes are insufficient to correct this, then the state must step in, taking ownership of the school system as necessary, closing it if necessary, and arranging for the transferal of the students to other districts or to charter schools. This will be hugely controversial, but after decades of complaining about school shortcomings nothing else has worked. The problems still exist in some school districts. Incompetent teachers are protected by tenure. Teachers still pay for supplies out of their own pockets. Children start and finish their school day in dirty, unhealthy facilities. Contrary to arguments made by those who don't want to spend the money, that "throwing more money at the problem doesn't work," it will work, if enough is thrown and in the right directions.

The first direction is in primary and secondary education though:

- More supplies
- Adequate non teaching staff, e.g. counselors, assistants and nurses
- Clean modern adequately sized, well lit, well-heated, ventilated and air conditioned facilities

The second direction is also in primary and secondary education:

- Teachers paid, not just adequately, but at a level that compensates them for doing the most important and essential job in the community. School Boards that don't already do so, must offer high pay and benefits that ensure teachers can afford to live in or close to their school district, in upper middle class housing as befits the status that they should have, without spending an exorbitant percentage of their pay for housing. Earnings should be in the order of median pay in the area for the most highly skilled workers. In return, the union must be forced to revise tenure to ensure that teachers not meeting a standard set by the Board can be efficiently terminated.

Some of the wealthier districts are already accomplishing much of this including appropriate salaries and excellent retirement benefits for teachers, but can these same improvements be accomplished within existing inner city and other disadvantaged economic settings?

Probably yes in some cases, no in others. Upgrading the schools may have to be accompanied by comparable upgrading, via public private partnership and low-income housing in the communities, so that before and after the school day our students benefit from adequate housing.

But they must of course have the benefit of adequate family support, and this will be addressed in Chapter Seven.

The third and last piece related to government funding, municipal, state or federal, relates to higher education:
- Federally funded two-year college tuition credit based on ability to pay—I will leave it at that for now; the value of the two-year degree and its relation to employability will be enhanced by the addition of the lessons in living curriculum, as you will read in Chapter Seven.

Looking at the Goals from the Perspectives of Others

Let me expand a little on the goals that I mentioned above in simplest terms—to give everyone the opportunity to achieve for them and their family the standard of living that I described—and to sufficiently enlighten them to truly participate in "government by the people" and to hold their elected officials at all levels accountable for their decisions and actions. And, as I have indicated, this can be done without a four-year degree, or for some careers without even a two-year degree. How do or did others look at these same goals?

Vermont Senator Bernie Sanders, when campaigning for the Democratic nomination for President in the run-up to the 2020 elections, said that we must ensure for all a quality education, living wages, affordable housing, healthcare and a secure retirement. We must take the global leadership in climate control and reducing pollution.[1] He was implying a heavily regulated society/economy, be it capitalist or socialist, nationalist or globalist, Independent, Republican or Democrat, I think that while we might not agree with Bernie's social-democrat approach to guaranteeing the benefits with no strings attached, we do agree that this is the type of America for which we should strive, the disagreement being on the degree of regulation. And major political movements over the years have made great strides in achieving this.

President Lincoln wrote to Congress in 1861 that the purpose of the federal government was "to elevate the condition of men, to lift artificial burdens from all shoulders, and to give everyone an unfettered start and a fair chance in the race of life." His actions to this end included the Homestead Act in that year distributing approximately 10 percent of all the land in the country to western settlers in 160-acre pieces.[2]

The Progressives of the early 20th century championed by Teddy Roosevelt and his Square Deal reduced the corrupt influence of the political bosses, promoted social programs, and regulated banking and corporate interests, all to the benefit of the working man.

Franklin Roosevelt at the Democratic Party's convention in 1936 said that "Liberty requires opportunity to make a living—a living decent according to the standard of the time, a living which gives man not only enough to live by, but something to live for." And he took action in that direction with the New Deal programs. Later came Lyndon Johnson with his Great Society producing Medicare and Medicaid, making health care available to millions more Americans.

Yes, we've achieved a lot and have whittled away at poverty. Real wages have steadily risen in spite of some claims to the contrary, and our high-tech tools have surely contributed to a better quality of life for all. Yet, in spite of these efforts, the opportunity to reach this goal of a living wage and decent quality of life still alludes many of us in the "soft underbelly" of our nation. Hundreds of thousands of Americans are homeless. Millions barely get by on food and health care because they spend half their income on rent. "Had individual income kept pace with overall economic growth since 1970, Americans in the bottom 90 percent of the income distribution would be making an extra $12,000 per year on average."[2]

Chapter Three
Vote—My Vote Does Count!

> *My dear friends: Your vote is precious,*
> *almost sacred. It is the most power-*
> *ful nonviolent tool we have to create a*
> *more perfect union.*
>> John Lewis, 2012 voting speech
>> in Charlotte, North Carolina

Let's look again at what should make/keep America great...first...exceptional.

We are not "great" now. We may be the best, and we can make a case that we still are. But no nation, certainly no democracy, that claims to be governed by "we the people" can claim to be a great nation when one third or more of its eligible voters don't exercise their right to vote, a right for which our founders and those who followed have fought and died.

What is the greatest freedom that we enjoy, perhaps the one factor that most separates the free world from the oppressed—the right to vote, to freely express ourselves at the polls. But that's only part of it. With these rights come responsibilities and here we fall short. In 2020 with an enormous effort on both sides to get out the vote, only approximately 66 percent of eligible voters cast ballots. This was touted as a great achievement by the American people because, up until 2020, in presidential elections typically only 60 percent of us turned out, in midterms only 40 percent. The media looked at this as the glass being "two thirds full." I look at the glass as being "one third empty." Why do one third of us eligible to vote still choose not to? Reasons abound, from apathy, ignorance regarding the issues, despair, mistrust of the system, mistrust of the candidates, or voter suppression by one side. How is it possible that so many of us, some benefiting from abundant opportunities and an enviable standard of living, some left behind but struggling to get ahead, fall into these categories and sit on the sidelines?

If we are ever to regain our role as the leader of the free world, more of us must come off the sidelines, educate ourselves on the issues and step into the voting booth. And beware, those of us who think we know for whom and for what we are voting don't always really understand the candidates and their policies because we are victims of an all too pervasive confirmation bias. We tend to get most of our news from only the sources with whom we agree, the sources that confirm our preferences and biases. The media plays to this and the candidates link hands with the media of their choice. The resultant groups of voters, media and politicians on each side become more entrenched, more divided, and more aggressive in their opposition to the extreme positions of the other party, the positions that really separate them from the other side. Liberals and Conservatives alike are tarred with the same brushes used on those who promote these most extreme positions. Dialog becomes almost impossible as we search our favorite news sources for anything that will refute the claims of the other side. Dialog and compromise in Congress both follow and reinforce the positions of the constituents. An endless destructive and obstructive circle!

In two successive presidential elections, 2016 and 2020, roughly half of the voters chose Donald Trump, a man whom the other half saw as an incompetent businessman who had made a career of bankruptcies, scamming creditors, avoiding taxes, defending lawsuits and ripping off his subcontractors, a narcissist who would go on from day one in office to make a habit of lying to his constituents about his accomplishments, alienating us from our allies, cozying up to our enemies, insulting disadvantaged nations, bullying others who cannot defend themselves, and destroying the planet?

Those who saw only his shortcomings couldn't imagine voting for him regardless of any of his accomplishments or any of his policies with which they might agree.

However, those who voted for Donald Trump, many of whom were fully aware of his moral deficit and other inadequacies, supported and still support him based on their traditional Republican views favoring small government, a free market economy and conservative social values and/or one or more overriding issues that determined their votes in 2016 and/or 2020. Those issues to them include the absolute necessity of a right leaning Supreme Court that would support a right to life agenda, and an almost fanatical opposition to the party that they see supporting the excesses of the Green New Deal and other social benefits derived from increased taxes and other wealth transfers, e.g. guaranteed minimum income, free college tuition for all, and forgiveness of college tuition debt, that will move us further along a road to socialism while bankrupting the country—a party that they see fostering some of the absurdities of our concerns with political correctness and the stifling of free speech especially in academia—a party that has turned wokeness into a way of life and blames all of society's ills on systemic racism.

Then too, while most of the benefits of the 2017 tax cut went to the upper echelon, the Trump supporters argue correctly that it also benefitted the working class. And it's hard to deny that, while no benefits have yet been achieved from Trump's stand on China, he did raise the awareness of the challenge and perhaps laid the groundwork for the Biden administration to deal with it—also his administration appears to have taken a real step toward improved relations between Israel and the Arab states—and I think we all favor and are impressed with his ridding the world of the top Iranian General, Soleimani and the leader of the Islamic State in Iraq, al-Baghdadi. There are, of course, other reasons for voting for Trump that his supporters give, notably his roles in expediting COVID-19 vaccine development and changing immigration policies.

Having said all this, we really didn't have a good choice in 2020, did we—either vote for a party led by a candidate with significant moral shortcomings or a party heavily influenced by its extreme liberal element viewed as leading us down a path to socialism.

We must overcome our confirmation bias and better educate ourselves on the strengths and shortcomings of the candidates and the rationale and excesses of the platforms, if we hope to nominate better qualified candidates with more universally acceptable platforms. Then, if we diligently vote in both the primaries and the elections, we can look forward to nominations and election outcomes that we can all support, or at least accept, in spite of our differences—outcomes that will join us instead of divide us.

But aside from the specific issues that concern the voters more attuned to them, there are as many, if not more, voters, many, socially or economically disadvantaged, who cast their ballots based on their identity with a certain social and/or economic group and what they perceive in general to be the advantages of one political party over the other for that group. And it was all too easy for the elites and other Democrats to negatively generalize these groups and fail to give them their due when campaigning. Hillary Clinton so obtusely expressed her feeling, much to her regret as it likely cost her the 2016 election, by implying that some of these Trump supporters are simply the "deplorables."

Deplorable? Really? How do so many of them ply a trade, or, lacking a trade, survive on meager earnings that barely enable them to put food on the table? How do they manage to raise a family, look out for their neighbors, maintain a house, repair their vehicles, participate in their town meetings and other community events and organizations? How do so many of them have the entrepreneurial spirit to overcome their financial challenges and start their small community businesses, many of which grow to achieve significance in a much larger market. Much of this is alien to many of the "elite" class. The answers are quite obvious. The main difference between the members of the different classes is not in their inherent intelligence but rather in the social and economic umbrella under which they were born and the educational opportunities available to them.

Let's look at many of the less advantaged who have been left behind in pursuit of the American dream. They may live in inner cities where access to quality schooling does not exist. They may live in rural areas where access to trustworthy news does not exist. Many rely on the unending stream of misinformation fed to them by Facebook, Twitter and other unreliable social media magnified by word of mouth throughout their community, just as we all would do were we not familiar with or did not have access to *The Economist, The Washington Post, Wall Street Journal* or other reliable publications or news sources, left leaning, right leaning or neutral.

When searching for "expert" advice, they may rely on their evangelical leaders, who may, in the name of their God, implore them to support the pro-life movement at all costs, including the millions of dollars that they pour into evangelical organizations, some of which seem to many of us more like cults than houses of worship. Then, when they really need an expert opinion, they quite understandably rely on the words of the national leader, their expert of last resort, who, in the words of a typical Trump follower that I heard quoted, "has access to information that we don't, and his tweets are always truthful."

Most of us seek and take comfort in some sort of identity. The upper class identifies with its prep schools and colleges, its clubs, and various community organizations. The disadvantaged, specifically disadvantaged white males, would be more apt to identify with the above-mentioned evangelical groups or with some of the self identified as "patriotic" organizations that favor "America First" and may not include immigrants and others that do not look or act like them. They join a culture of those who respect and consider themselves part of a tribe of strong, self sufficient, hard working individuals who are not going to be told how to run their lives or how to communicate in politically correct terms. Viewing them being interviewed at Trump rallies, most of them, with the exception of the really hard core white supremacists and domestic terrorists, resemble their liberal counterparts, albeit less masked in pandemic times, and they speak for their cause as fervently as those speaking in opposition. The ultimate, as the Trump term expired, was in their seemingly total agreement on one unarguable "truth," the election was rigged and the results a fraud. Based on Trump's continuing daily tweets over the months of the campaign and the aftermath of the election, it seems that they either believed this falsehood all along, they became so brainwashed and so desirability biased that they came to believe it, or, while they didn't really believe the theory, they got a kick out of joining others in yelling out their support for the theory, not realizing the serious consequences of their action. At the extreme of course, there were also some who can only be described as domestic terrorists as evidenced by their acts of violence on January 6 while storming and temporarily occupying the Capitol.

Regardless of the above, the raw material, what we are made of, is pretty much the same for all of us, the less advantaged and the more fortunate, including those who support Donald Trump and those who do not. The difference is in the outside forces frequently out of our control, where we were born and how the community of our birthplace educated and set an example for us.

Let's examine how we can revise the system and enlighten and encourage us all to participate in this government "by the people," not just by voting, but by staying tuned to the values of our representative democracy and the needs and aspirations of our communities, neighbors, institutions, nation and planet.

This can be done. Currently, we vote if we are passionate enough about an issue to make the effort, witness the increased turnout for the 2020 presidential election, or perhaps more significant, the large turnout in the 2020 Wisconsin primaries standing in long lines for in some cases hours right at the peak of the Covid-19 pandemic—risking health for their cause. In presidential elections, even in mid-terms, there are multiple causes affected by the vote. It's simply a matter of educating the public to the point that they are more aware of them.

Excuses, Excuses, Why Don't We Vote?
Now we all have excuses, some understandable, but none justified. What are some of them, and what can we do about it?

- **The game is rigged**, so my vote doesn't count. With the exception of gerrymandering, which is of course a "rigging" method, there is no evidence to support this.

  We must educate our voters accordingly in one of our lessons, and strict controls should be applied to the geography and demographics of Congressional districts.

- **Money talks**. The candidate with the most money, either his or her own, or more likely raised by wealthy benefactors turned oligarchs, wins. Often, but not always true. We must get the dollars out of the elections, but how?

End Citizens United, a Supreme Court ruling in Citizens United v. Federal Election Commission stating that corporations and other outside groups can spend unlimited money on elections if they are not formally coordinating with a particular candidate or political party.

Impose strict Congressional term limits, e.g. three terms for Representatives and two for Senators, to drastically reduce the percentage of the total time during their career in office spent raising funds to support re-election.

The failure to vote can result from apathy, but also from impediments placed on the voting public to ensure that voting regulations favor the party in power.

The one overarching failure can only be traced to how and to what end we educate ourselves. And here I am not talking about, or even considering, the financial impediments to a college education and the progressive moves to eliminate these impediments. In fact, I am not even considering college education as part of, or at least a significant part of, the education issue.

Starting with childhood, the three key elements of the education that we all need in order to become enlightened citizens are:

- Learning to communicate, i.e. read, write and converse at the earliest age with parental guidance or other mentoring that encourages reading as an integral part, preferably a passionate part, of daily life

- Exposure to, and tolerance of, the thoughts and opinions of others from diverse backgrounds
- Instruction in the non-academic and nonscientific subjects that lead to a productive, and enlightened life, what I have termed lessons in living

These and their relationship to technical training, apprenticeships, and primary, secondary and higher education will be addressed in Chapter Seven.

Follow me as I lay out the path that will provide a foundation that defines our objectives and long term goals on which to base our decisions when we cast our votes.

Voting and Joining

Those who pitch in and participate in social and civic enterprises for the benefit of the community vote. Those who vote participate. A century ago, many civic organizations were founded and existed to address the nation's problems—the Food and Drug Administration, the Forest Service, the suffrage movement, the Federal Reserve, Boy Scouts, 4-H, etc. Four amendments to the U.S. Constitution were passed. In the 1930s the New Deal agencies were created. In the 1940s, the United Nations, NATO, the World Bank and the IMF came into being.[3] Why are we not able to build something new and comparable in today's social and political climate? Unfortunately, we have become so polarized that overcoming our differences and making the compromises required to create a meaningful new civic institution are difficult, if not impossible.[3]

However, I think we are finally seeing some hope as exemplified by the bipartisan support that we are seeing for a massive new civic institution, universal national service!

This institution, like any other of significant benefit, needs a foundation of overall goals along the lines of those to which I have already referred. And, as a basis for these goals, ideally we need a national mission for today and vision for tomorrow.

Our mission and our vision must consider the needs of the individual, the needs of the nation and the needs of the globe, and should be the basis for the decisions that we make when we enter the voting booth. Suggestions about how the mission and vision might be developed and drafted are included in Chapter Six.

Chapter Four
Good Citizens

> *Each time a man stands up for an ideal, or acts to improve the lot of others, or strikes out against injustice, he sends forth a tiny ripple of hope, and crossing each other from a million different centers of energy and daring, these ripples build a current that can sweep down the mightiest walls of oppression and resistance.*
> Robert Kennedy speech,
> Cape Town, June 6, 1966

Five years ago, when I first gave some serious thought to what would be required to overcome our malaise, something really revolutionary, I asked my readers a question that I had previously asked myself, "Do you believe that our wars over the past five decades (now six) or so have all been justified and well-managed, and that our electorate is sufficiently enlightened and engaged regarding the management of our nation's social and economic problems to sustain 'government by the people?'" If their answer was in the negative, I suggested they read on, as I made a case in *Step Forward America!* for a universal national service program that, as I pointed out in Chapter One would:

- Involve everyone in providing the services—military or civilian—required to keep our country great, to support our values and traditions, to keep us safe from outside threats, to participate in governing, in other words to have some skin in the game

- Expose everyone to the culture and opinions of others from all backgrounds in order to make them more capable of meeting these ends
- Educate and enlighten ourselves to further these goals

By accomplishing these, we can turn our youth and all of us into good citizens, not just good students or good athletes. David Epstein in a Wall Street Journal opinion piece summed up good citizenship when he said that the bedrock principles and values that he would like to pass on to his descendants were "integrity is not negotiable; never stop learning; cling to the aspirations of the Declaration of Independence and defend the restraints of the Constitution; and salute the flag....Oh, and ask substantive questions."[4] David Brooks in a New York Times article drew from the 19th century English philosopher John Stuart Mill when he wrote that real citizenship involves understanding how to separate good from evil, and the rigorous from the sloppy, and reaching out to join those who serve others regardless of their backgrounds and beliefs.[5]

It is often said a good citizen charts and lives a life committed to self betterment while expressing and acting on communal, national and global concerns.[6]

Serve America Together

When I first envisioned a universal national service program, others were promoting a similar program, drawing on the ideas espoused by William F. Buckley in his 1990 book *Gratitude—Reflections On What We Owe To Our Country,* and influenced by other authors and pundits from the past. Taking the lead in this effort was the Franklin Project, a creation of the Aspen Institute that subsequently aligned with two other similarly motivated groups, Service Nation at Be The Change and the Service Year Exchange, to form Service Year Alliance headed up then and now by General Stanley McChrystal, former commander of forces in the Middle East and arguably our number one steward of national service. Service Year Alliance now leads a coalition in the campaign to make universal national service a reality, under the aptly named campaign label "Serve America Together." As mentioned in Chapter One, the National Commission on Military, National and Public Service was established in 2017 to study and report back to the President, Congress and the people on the support for a such a program. Their efforts and latest findings are presented on their website *Inspire2serve.gov*, and their final report, *Inspired to Serve,* was presented to the President, Congress and the American people March 25, 2020. Here is the essence of the Commission's report recommending a voluntary universal service program encompassing military, national, and public service:

"Service—beginning at an early stage and continuing throughout one's lifetime—develops skills and leadership among those who participate" and "helps develop the Nation's workforce; and brings people together to meet the critical needs of the Nation. Perhaps most importantly, enhancing the country's culture of service holds the promise of invigorating civic life in America and strengthening the foundation of the Republic."[7]

"In the course of its work, the Commission identified a major flaw in the American educational system: the lack of exposure to high-quality civic education for students throughout much of the Nation....When 22 percent of American adults cannot name any of the three branches of government, it is well past time for the country to take action. Significantly greater Federal investment in civic education....and incorporation of service learning within school curricula are critical to preparing young Americans to realize their obligation as citizens and expose them to opportunities to engage in military, national, and public service."[7]

Based on the findings, I'm happy to report that, as I previously mentioned, there are bills before both houses of Congress promoting national service by increasing funding for AmeriCorps Vista and other volunteer organizations that hopefully will have solid bi-partisan support.

So, what's so revolutionary about the program recommended by the Commission, you might ask. Don't we have plenty of voluntary programs right now... AmeriCorps VISTA, the Peace Corps, Senior Corps, etc.? Well, yes, we do have plenty of voluntary opportunities, but there is nowhere near adequate funding for these programs to accommodate the number of those wishing to participate. But more significantly, the universal program to be proposed will hopefully have enough carrots and sticks—i.e. benefits to participation and penalties for non-participation—that it will eventually, perhaps a generation or more from now, be truly universal, *de facto* mandatory. For example, with American academia on board, there can be tuition and course credits for those with a Service Year certificate. With corporate America on board, those with a Service Year certificate could go to the head of the recruiting line. And those not choosing to participate might not be eligible for certain Federal retirement benefits and tax advantages offered to those with a Certificate.

Voluntary versus Mandatory

Unfortunately, however, there are still some—two to be specific—important drawbacks to a voluntary versus mandatory program. In short, the voluntary program really only addresses one of the three goals identified at the beginning of this chapter, these goals being getting everyone involved, exposing them to others of diverse backgrounds, and educating and enlightening them in good citizenship, as discussed in *Step Forward America!* While the voluntary program addresses the first of these, getting everyone involved, the Commission's report does not recommend built-in basic training and education components and therefore does not adequately address the other two goals related to education and diversity. And so, as indicated in Chapter One, we will have to provide other opportunities throughout the primary, secondary and higher education pathway for these, and tailor the national service program to include a mandatory basic training period in order to provide for the benefits of living, learning and working together with others of diverse backgrounds.

Chapter Five
Amending our Traditional Education Model

> *Education is the most powerful weapon, which you can use to change the world.*
>
> *Nelson Mandela speech,*
> *Boston, June 23, 1990*

Our democracy never will reach its full potential until we are all educated enough to ensure that we have a thorough grasp of the issues and that we express our opinions throughout participation in our various communities and in the voting booth. This can only result from a life constantly exposed to learning opportunities of which we enthusiastically, even passionately, take advantage.

We should be placing the highest priority of education in preparing us for our civic responsibilities and for productive and enjoyable employment that affords us a standard of living providing us and our family the basics of adequate food, shelter and healthcare, and time for the pursuit of happiness.

In very general terms, the courses taught in our traditional academic or trade school curricula fall into three categories. First, there are the basic humanities and sciences. Second are the "trades," offered as an alternate at both the secondary and higher levels for those not suited to a liberal arts and sciences curriculum or for those who favor following a seamless school to career path much as old time apprentices prepared for their life long careers. And third would be courses centered around the previously mentioned lessons in living designed to prepare students to survive and even prosper in the increasingly challenging social and economic climate of our time. In our current education system, some of these are being adequately addressed in certain states and districts, others only minimally if at all. We need a whole new focus here.

This third education category must be blended with significant focus into our traditional education model starting with the formative years, and then also strongly reinforced in a mandatory basic training term in a universal national service program.

I do not live in academia, I do not have any degrees in education, and I am not suggesting anything like discarding the common core standards or a complete overhaul of any phase of our current education system. Rather, as a layman, I am merely recommending additional focus on certain aspects of existing curricula and the addition of some courses with our lessons in living that address the social, political and cultural environment in which we all live and with which we all wrestle.

In very simplest terms, early childhood and pre-K would include some of the very basic introduction to our lessons outlined in Chapter Six; for example, some "caring and courtesy" and perhaps some of the personal responsibility aspects covered in some of the other courses. Surely in today's climate we can all see the need to start focusing on personal responsibilities, specifically those related to understanding and telling the truth, at the earliest possible age. K through 8 through high school would continue to focus on basic mathematics, but not only focus on as they do now, but increase, where possible, required courses in reading, writing and speaking skills. And now we would add exposure to all, and mastery of some, of the Chapter Six "Lessons in Living." With these 13 years of required schooling, we would be well on the way to being prepared for our civic responsibilities and for productive and enjoyable employment, presumably significantly better prepared by the addition of these lessons than we are now. History, in addition to the American history included in the Civics courses, the physical and social sciences, and the other lessons currently taught in these years would fill up the schedule but most would be electives rather than required.

Two years of community college, possibly one "special curriculum" year of community college or the first two years of a four-year college could be other opportunities for courses that include our lessons for those who were not able to complete them in high school.

More specific details of where and when to teach these lessons are presented in Chapter Seven.

With or without some college, we are now better prepared to accept our civic responsibilities, as well as an offer for gainful employment by companies and other organizations in many administrative and support functions. We also would have a more sound foundation for many skilled jobs in companies that routinely provide training in the specific skills the jobs call for, or even in those companies who reluctantly provide training while complaining that they can't find applicants already fully trained.

Trade school or apprenticeships would, of course, further the employability for some of those jobs requiring specific skills.

The Experts Speak Out on the Value of Education

Let's look at what the experts consider the fundamentals of a sound education program, and start thinking about how our new focus might fit in, and how we would measure up.

In their book *That Used To Be Us,* Thomas Friedman and Michael Mandelbaum identify the four challenges that will shape America's future: "how to adapt to globalization, how to adjust to the information technology (IT) revolution, how to cope with the large and soaring budget deficits stemming from the growing demand on government at every level, and how to manage a world of both rising energy consumption and rising climate threats."[8] The authors go on to say that "America built the world's most vibrant economy and democracy precisely because, in every historical turn since its founding, it has applied its own unique formula for prosperity."[9]

Friedman and Mandelbaum describe the formula as consisting "of five pillars that together constitute the country's own version of a partnership between the public and private sectors to foster economic growth. The first pillar is providing public education for more and more Americans. As technology has improved, the country has prepared people to exploit new inventions — from cotton gins, to steamships, to assembly lines, to laptops, to the Internet."[9] This first pillar is, in my mind, the key to all the rest. Without the optimal effort here, we fall further and further behind. And most assuredly, for all the reasons we have stated, our lessons will contribute to this effort.

Friedman and Mandelbaum describe the other four pillars as continuing improvement of our infrastructure, keeping our doors to immigration open, government support of research and development, and regulating private economic activity including safeguards against financial collapse and environmental destruction.[9] These last four pillars all rely on the support of the first pillar as a strong everevolving educational element.

Friedman and Mandelbaum go on to talk about what employers need today: "They are looking for workers who can think critically, who can tackle non-routine complex tasks, and who can work collaboratively with teams located in their office or globally."[10] Surely our lessons, whether part of a national service program or learned elsewhere, will help young men and women achieve these competencies and be prepared to put them to use when they enter the work force.

James Speth takes a similar view, writing in *America the Possible,* "America can succeed only if it develops a powerful capacity to define and execute meaningful plans for dealing with complex challenges such as climate change and energy sector transformation...Planning requires, above all, competence—competence in government, in the private sector, and in citizens generally. And this competence in turn requires, above all, education and public integrity. Education is essential not just to build the skills needed in today's high-tech economy, but also to build a capacious understanding of the world in which we live."[11]

This education must include both traditional (albeit hopefully greatly improved) book learning, pre-K through high school and beyond, and the broader education in understanding and facing the challenges of the twenty-first century, much of which should come from our lessons in living.

In his book *How Children Succeed*, Paul Tough, a former editor of the *New York Times Magazine*, states that

teaching math and reading to children, especially disadvantaged children, isn't enough. We should also be teaching the non-cognitive skills, i.e. "character," what it takes to have a successful life, not just good school grades.[12]

Jeff Nelson, who runs high school programs called "One Goal" in Chicago, aimed at improving student achievement and college acceptance, describes these traits, or leadership skills as he calls them, as "resilience, integrity, resourcefulness, and ambition and says that "They are the linchpin of what we do."[12]

Tough goes on to state that these skill can even be taught to teenagers from difficult backgrounds who have not benefitted from childhood training, and they can then be better equipped to strive for a better life.[12]

Character traits of resilience, integrity, resourcefulness and ambition abound in our lessons. Supposedly, the Duke of Wellington credited England's victory over Napoleon's armies at the Battle of Waterloo to lessons learned "on the playing fields of Eton." Friedman and Mandelbaum echo that sentiment when they write in *That Used to be Us,* "one could argue that the stability and prosperity of the twenty-first century international order will be maintained—or lost—in the classrooms of America's public schools."[13] But if winning, not losing, is our preference, then vast improvements will be required. Some of those improvements can surely be achieved through our lessons.

Now envisioning these lessons being taught in our traditional education process, they will be reinforced in the mandatory basic training term of a universal national service program. Content in the basic training would be presented in book form or online, or more likely some combination, with brief supplementary lectures by volunteer mentors, possibly from Senior Corps, who provide recruits with an opportunity for discussion and deeper personal engagement. At the conclusion of each Life Prep course, a recommended reading list would be handed out with discounted prices for both paperback and electronic versions, making it relatively easy for our participants to further their education in these subjects voluntarily and on their own.

The Nordic Model

I would hope that the new focus on "lessons in living" in our schools and in our national service basic training would lead us in the direction outlined by David brooks in his article "This Is How Scandinavia Got great." It would mirror the results of the Nordic model. Sweden, Denmark, Norway and Finland generally excel in economic productivity, social equality, social trust and personal happiness. In the 19th century, they realized that, if they were to prosper, they would have to develop a system that enhances the standards of even the least educated, and that life long learning would be the social norm. They described this process using the German word "bildung" that encompasses the "complete moral, emotional, intellectual and civic transformation of the person" in order to both benefit from and contribute to their emerging industrial society.[14]

While we in America tend to look at education as the transmission of certain skills, the Nordic model is geared to teaching students how to see the world in terms of the relationships between self, family, friends, community, and society in general, and how to take responsibility for and enjoy their role. They realize that we go through phases as we grow, responding to different authorities, and developing our own norms and values.

All of this contributes to an environment with the lowest corruption in the world and a society that understands and accepts the right balance between individual freedoms and communal responsibility.[14] Let's just look at one example demonstrating how we in America fall short on this balance. In March 2020 when the coronavirus pandemic was hitting us with full force, the authorities, federal and state, were all recommending, if not mandating, that we all make social distancing a part of our normal routine. In fact it was widely thought that social distancing was the practice most critical to minimizing exposure, sickness and death. At first, while it seemed that the younger generation was really not too susceptible to a serious case of the virus, it was widely known by all, including them, that, if infected, they could readily expose the much more susceptible older generation, their grandparents for example, to the virus. Regardless, college student spring breakers flocked to Miami and the beaches to party just as they always do at that time of year, just as if the pandemic didn't exist. No concern for their safety or their friends' safety, understandable perhaps, but not acceptable—no concern for the possibility that they might carry and transmit the virus to those with limited resistance, the seniors, their grandparents, or perhaps even their parents included. And how about giving a little thought to those overworked essential workers in health care putting their lives on the line constantly exposed to the virus while caring for some patients that were hospitalized due to their complete failure to follow the recommended common sense precautions of masking, self distancing, and minimizing exposure to crowds.

This was not solely a matter of ignorance. They were subject to fierce criticism in the media, but that didn't seem to matter. Later, in the fall when some colleges and universities opened up in-person courses on campus with strict precaution to control the virus, many of the students ignored the precautions and participated in the typical college party scene with the expected results, the spread of the virus causing the colleges to reconsider and shutdown on campus in-person classes.[15] How can this be? Well apparently these students either skipped the classes in their lifelong learning that dealt with responsibility to the community, or the teachers, from parents to professors, didn't offer the class, or they themselves didn't have the background to teach it.

I think we can assume that the three Scandinavian countries, Denmark, Norway and Finland, that have had much lower COVID-19 death rates than the United States, can attribute much of their success to their above mentioned focus on teaching students how to see the world in terms of the relationships between self, family, friends, community, and society in general, and how to take responsibility for their role. This would seem to be in direct contrast to the behavior of some of our college students. I have excluded Sweden from these comments because they took a different approach to the pandemic, electing to minimize shutdowns, and consequently they suffered much higher death rates than their neighbors.

Knowledge and Skill Versus Oil, Gas and Diamonds

In Tom Friedman's *New York Times* column "Pass the Books. Hold the Oil," he quotes Andreas Schleicher, director of the Program for International Student Assessment (PISA) for the Organization for Economic Cooperation and Development. Schleicher observes that "today's learning outcomes at school are a powerful predictor for the wealth and social outcomes that countries will reap in the long run."[16] He cites as excellent examples Finland, Singapore, Hong Kong, South Korea, and Japan, all countries with few natural resources. In those countries "education has strong outcomes and a high status, at least in part because the public at large has understood that the country must live by its knowledge and skills and that these depend on the quality of its education....Every parent and child in these countries knows that these skills will decide the life chances of the child and nothing else is going to rescue them, so they build a whole culture and education system around it."[16]

Friedman goes on: " 'In sum,' says Schleicher, 'knowledge and skills have become the global currency of 21st century economics, but there is no central bank that prints this currency. Everyone has to decide on their own how much they will print.' Sure, it's great to have oil, gas and diamonds; they can buy jobs. But they'll weaken your society in the long run unless they're used to build schools and a culture of life long learning. 'The thing that will keep you moving forward,' says Schleicher, is always 'what you bring to the table yourself.'"[16]

Breaking the Roadblocks to Income Equality
Columnist David Brooks is concerned that populist progressives often blame income inequality on the private economy's failure to generate jobs and on political and corporate power roadblocks. In Brooks' view, the real problem is the lack of appropriate worker skills. He calls for government to expand early education, expand worker training and provide better and more affordable community colleges, as keys to the most effective way to improve the readiness and productivity of our workforce.[17]

Our lessons are not only compatible with, but an integral part of, any improvement in our educational system that will keep us "moving forward" in the words of Andreas Schleicher and "improve the readiness and productivity of our workforce" as expressed by Mr. Brooks.

Apparently the independent, nonpartisan think tank, the Council on Foreign Relations, agrees. Their statistics consistently show the United States lagging behind most of our global peers in reading, basic math skills and sciences. They show us failing to prepare sufficient workers to meet the needs of our life-sciences and aerospace industries as well as the needs of our State Department and intelligence agencies. Perhaps even more revealing, the CFR notes that our educational shortcomings also disqualify a significant number of our 17to 24-yr-olds from even joining the military. Further, our shortcomings in civics training are leaving our students inadequately prepared for the duties of basic citizenship.[18]

The countries that excel seem to be those that hold the teaching profession in higher regard, those that focus more on the neediest students, have a higher percentage in high quality pre-school, have a culture of constant improvement, and apply rigorous standards throughout. This last requirement seems to be the only one that we have tried to address and its use has been met with a great deal of controversy and pushback. Known as The Common Core State Standards Initiative, it defines the knowledge and skills students should gain throughout their K-12 years in order to graduate high school prepared to succeed in entry-level careers, introductory academic college courses, and workforce training programs. At one point, Common Core had been fully adopted by 36 states and the District of Columbia, 10 other states were either making major revisions or adopting only a part of the Common Core, and four states had rejected the Common Core from the time it was introduced in 2009. And there is some ongoing backlash: President Trump and his education secretary Betsy DeVos had called for a blanket repeal of the Common Core. In the light of the PISA report, this resistance to raising educational standards, when student achievement in some states continues to be mediocre, is indeed regrettable.[19]

To be fair, the problems cited above cannot all be attributed to the shortcomings of our teachers and schools. There is a bigger societal problem that must be factored in. Obviously, students from stable homes with an environment conducive to inquiring and learning, where English is the language spoken, where parents are more educated, where they involve themselves in the daily routines of their children, and where they have reading material available to them and their children, do better on average regardless of the curriculum standards.[20] I will address this in Chapter Seven, as it relates to early childhood learning, but it applies equally to primary and secondary education.

In 2011, the Council on Foreign Relations sponsored an independent study of the relationship between national security and the poor performance of America's students. The task force, made up of 31 prominent education experts, national security authorities, and corporate leaders, including former Secretary of State Condoleezza Rice and former chancellor of New York

City Public Schools system Joel I. Klein, made three priority recommendations for reform:

- The Common Core standards should be adopted and expanded, with focus on subjects vital to the national security.
- Students and their parents should be given more choice in where they go to school and resources should be allocated equitably to ensure that good educational opportunities are available to all.
- A national security readiness audit should be implemented; the public should be made aware of the results and the schools and policy makers should be held accountable.[21]

Some of this is now being addressed, but what the final course of action, if any, will be remains to be seen. Contrary to what some pundits tell us, however, we must indeed throw additional money at our lackluster educational system, but it must be directed at higher qualified teachers, adequate nonteaching staffs, supplies and facilities, and financial support for two years of college tuition.

Salvage Operation

Let's make sure that our whole education system is structured so that those who are indeed suited to, and wish to, can go on to a two or four year college education. Those who are not—and there are clearly many in this category—can be directed to a path preparing them for manufacturing jobs, the manual trades, health care technician work, clerical work, retail sales, food service, personal care, etc. and other working class jobs that can support them and their family. Vocational education should be directed more toward manufacturing, the manual trades and the higher end of the service sector, i.e. health and education, many of which jobs require some technical skills, so that fewer members gravitate toward lower paying, lower skills labor in food service and personal and property care. According to a McKinsey report published in 2016, a full 79 percent of work activities are susceptible or somewhat susceptible to automation and the education system will have to continually adjust for these trends.[22]

That said, there are some steps that can be taken to alleviate the plight of some of the lowest paid of our workforce right now. For example, we should raise the minimum wage for all, or even for specific service sectors such as fast-food workers, who represent a very large population. Contrary to public belief, most fast food workers are not high school students working part-time; rather, they are over 20 years old, often raising a child, and the job is the sole source of income for their families. They are also twice as likely to receive public assistance as are other working class families. Since 1938 when Franklin Roosevelt implemented a national minimum wage, periodic increases have not come close to keeping up with the cost of living. We're starting to correct this, but we can do more. If the minimum wages account for the cost of living in the locale, and are adjusted for tips where applicable, then, in the long run, the additional money in the hands of these workers and consumers should more than offset the loss of some jobs in businesses that cannot afford the hikes.[23]

We cannot go on producing poorly educated college grads, deeply in debt and incapable of gaining employment that truly requires a valid college degree. Caleb Rossiter in a *Wall Street Journal* column emphasized this point when he said that half the high school students in high poverty areas drop out, and the remaining who do manage to graduate, perform at only a fifth grade level. Only 10 percent of the ninth grade students that he taught in Washington DC were even in attendance more than three days a week, and those chronically absent ignored their class work and home work.[24] I believe a general lack of discipline underlies a great deal of our society's ills and, while it may start in the home, perhaps with a working mom and an absent dad, it is fostered in the education scenario just described. Surely "graduates" of our lessons in living curriculum will have a positive influence on this and start to swing the pendulum in the opposite direction.

We can also take a page from the European model of post-secondary education, increasing the opportunities for some kind of formal vocational education that could be an excellent transitional step between high school or national service and a good middle class job. In Germany, while high school graduates are much less likely to attend college than here, many more go on to vocational training. In fact, 85 percent of those employed in the private economy have had vocational training and have served an apprenticeship; their earnings average 92 percent of the average German wage.[25] While we push college as a goal for almost everyone, the truth is that college isn't a suitable fit for many. Many college graduates are not able to find employment in the fields for which they are trained, and, to make matters worse, they start their working career saddled with a mountain of college debt. Certainly for them, government-subsidized vocational training could be a better answer.

There are many callings where associate's degrees and professional certifications suffice. And, if the education to this point includes our lessons, that's another important step toward employability.

When Siemens manufacturing was unable to find enough workers with sufficient skills to operate its new gas and steam turbine manufacturing facility in Charlotte, North Carolina, it joined with other manufacturers in the state to develop a three-year apprenticeship program leading to an associate's degree and a $55,000 starting salary job.[26] Associate's degrees are in many places as valuable as bachelor's degrees. In Colorado, experienced associates of applied science have virtually the same earnings as their counterparts with bachelor's degrees, and in some fields—computer engineering technologies, building construction, and nursing for example— base earnings are actually higher.[27]

Chapter Six
Lessons in Living---A Common Core for a Citizen Corps

> *One child, one teacher, one book and one pen can change the world. Education is the only solution. Education first.*
> *Malala Yousafzai, speaking to the UN General Assembly in New York, July 12, 2013*

This Life Preparation curriculum is an expansion of that outlined in *Step Forward America!* and would include a core of a dozen or more lessons in living on which to focus, some already taught to a degree in some districts. Note that many, if not most, of these could elicit the passion of a student leading not only to a lifelong interest, but to a lifelong commitment. One more lesson The Art of Compromise, will be covered later in Chapter Nine.

Authors with Authority

Most of these subjects address issues with political overtones. Therefore, when developing the course, input must come from both conservative and liberal points of view, and this is critical to the value of these lessons. Experts in the field from both sides must write the lessons clearly demonstrating the opposing views and justifications for same. A national bipartisan commission should be appointed, or possibly elected, charged with appointing the authors of each lesson. This commission should be as independent as possible, with advise and consent from the Department of Education. And the commission should be charged with the task of ensuring that the output of these chosen authors be required in the education system across the nation, taking precedence over any local or state sponsored conflicting evangelical or other alternate versions of history—a tall order!

In addition to authors for each of these lessons, we will need additional academic expertise to address the place in the education process for introducing the material, as some of it might only be appropriate at the high school level, whereas some of the other lessons might be introduced sequentially starting as early as pre-K. These experts would presumably review the material and make recommendations to the authors to revise and rewrite as necessary the lessons making them appropriate for sequential introduction.

What follows are neither course outlines nor lesson plans, but just my opinions regarding what those who write the courses and plans should consider.

Arguably, the most critical of the courses would be Civics, and this must be taught extensively before the students reach voting age.

Civics

Over the past two administrations, trust in our federal government has reached an all time low. According to the Pew Research Center, a poll in 2019 indicated that only 17 percent of Americans trusted the federal government to do the right thing always or most of the time.[28] The conventional thinking was that, in the aftermath of the 2008 financial crisis, banks and corporations were bailed out while average people lost their homes. The upper and upper middle classes were doing fine but for the others who constitute the majority, while unemployment, at least until the time of the COVID-19 pandemic, was at an all time low, wages for many of them were far from adequate to meet a living wage standard. Yes, one could argue with some or all of this, but perception for the most part has become reality. Lacking trust in the government to do something, anything in many cases, and seeing Congress so incapacitated by partisan wrangling, is it any wonder that we have lost faith in our government? Why can't we fix this? Simply because most of us do not really understand how government functions or is supposed to function. Lacking this knowledge, we are not in a position to take corrective action. At the top of the list of our lessons should be a strong focus on civics so that everyone who recognizes shortcomings in how we govern ourselves will also understand the causes and be able to advocate for suitable solutions.

As I previously pointed out, the National Commission on Military, National and Public Service in their Final Report noted "a major flaw in the American educational system: the lack of exposure to high-quality civic education for students throughout much of the Nation."[29] Consequently, they recommend the creation of a Civic

Education Fund to "develop and implement best practice curricula that incorporate civic education, applied civics, and service learning across the K-12 experience" and a ServiceLearning Fund to "develop and implement servicelearning programs and opportunities for hands-on community service for K-12 and postsecondary students across the country."[30]

In the report, the Commission defines *civic education* to include "teaching the fundamental principles enshrined in the Constitution, Declaration of Independence, and other founding documents; deepening students' understanding of how those principles apply to civic life; and providing experiences that intentionally prepare students for informed, engaged participation in civic life."[31]

In our curriculum, however, the Civics lessons will also address American history focusing on our major wars and social movements and their relationship with the founding documents. We will highlight our international leadership and our extraordinary national progress as well as the set backs in meeting our challenges since the days of the original settlers. We will not gloss over our treatment of the native Americans, our reliance on slavery in building the country, and the subsequent unequal treatment of the black community. Nor will we allow wokeness and the cancel culture thinking to unduly focus on these failures.

The Commission's report defines *service learning* as "an instructional approach that integrates classroom teaching and reflection with community service projects. Service learning techniques may be applied in virtually any class including science and mathematics—and provide students with meaningful experiences by exposing them to the values of service, such as commitment, contribution to community, and collaboration."[31]

A federal report in 2011 indicated that only 7 percent of eighth graders could identify all three branches of government; only 24 percent of twelfth graders were proficient in the broader concepts of civics which has been defined as recognizing the complementary roles of citizens, government, nongovernmental organizations, and the private sector in building and maintaining a democratic society. Most Americans, asked to name the supreme law of the land, do not name the Constitution as their answer.[32] Many if not most of our high school graduates, or perhaps even college grads, would struggle with the oral test given to immigrants applying for naturalization. That test requires correct answers to six out of any ten questions taken from a list of 100 on history and civics. The poor showing of our nation's students will presumably improve somewhat based on the implementation of the Common Core Standards on primary and secondary school curricula. These standards, although very controversial when first proposed, and still somewhat controversial in many districts, have now been adopted by the majority of the 50 states.

Typical Common Core lesson plans for civics include teaching the fundamentals of our constitutional government as well as the meaning of the Declaration of Independence, the U.S. Constitution, and the Bill of Rights, all of which is vital. Steps currently being taken to incorporate more civics and government education in high school, as well as in some middle school curricula, are being aided by the Center for Civic Education which networks with the 50 states offering a course, "We the People—The Citizen and the Constitution" on the history and principles of the Constitution. Since its inception in 1987, about 3 million students and 75,000 educators have participated.[33]

This new focus would be reinforced in our civics education course. And as part of this course when studying the Constitution, I would recommend an exercise that would address the perceived shortcomings of the document created in the 18th century, as it applies to conditions in the 21st century unanticipated by the Founding Fathers. This could be a requirement for all students to draft amendments that they would propose. Possible new amendments might address the limitations, or lack of same, of the "right of the people to keep and bear arms" as set forth in the existing Amendment II, or a revision to the statement in Article I section 5 that authorizes each House to "determine the Rules of its Proceedings" this latter giving seemingly dictatorial powers to the Speaker of the House and Senate Majority Leader that contribute so heavily to the current roadblocks to legislation. Then again a consideration of eliminating the electoral college would also seem to be in order, especially in light of the excess attention given to the voters in the "swing states" in recent elections. Surely the process outlined in the Constitution, by the framers in considering the politics of the 18th century, does not ensure that all votes now carry equal weight.

Emphasis on civics should also lead to improved voter participation. In October 2013 the Commission on Youth Voting and Civic Knowledge released a report entitled "All Together Now: Collaboration and Innovation for Youth Engagement." The need for the study was underlined by the fact that the participation of young voters at the polls in 2012 was proportionately way below that of their elders. This pattern was similar in the 2016 elections, but reliable data is not yet available for 2020. The 2013 report pointed out that opportunity for civic learning in the home varies greatly between wealthy and low-income households. Much of this has to do with the frequency of parent-child discussions often around the dinner table and whether parents encourage their adolescent children to express opinions and disagreements. In low-income households there is often just less family time available for talking and watching news reports on TV. Also, while teachers face some opposition from the public about what is taught in civics, researchers have found that civics education works. In recommending new and better approaches to teaching civics, the researchers suggested lowering the voting age in municipal and state elections to 17, the age when students are typically studying civics in school, and implementing new state standards that require students to read and discuss news in class. Such a change should also stimulate such conversations with parents or other adults outside of the classroom.[34]

Our lessons in civics, as well as other lessons we offer in media literacy, should be a significant help in teaching students to examine some of their beliefs and prejudices more closely. I would hope that somewhere in this education process, the students would learn to be more tolerant of the opinions of others who disagree with them, and realize that most major political issues are not all black and white. A review of past and present government policies give us pause to think. Take for example the treatment of prisoners at Guantanamo. Did the end—the swift removal of suspected terrorists from society through imprisonment— justify the means, which included suspension of the Writ of Habeas Corpus, violations of the Geneva Conventions in regard to the physical treatment of prisoners, and condemnation from our allies? Or for those arguing against the excesses of the welfare state, should the people getting food stamps despite working full-time jobs be denied assistance if they are stuck in minimum wage jobs and still not earning enough to sustain their families? For those advocating right to life, are we talking about all unborn fetuses, even those resulting from incest and rape? Do these same proponents also regard as sacrosanct the life of a convicted murderer on death row? How do we feel about the lives of the innocent civilians killed by our drone strikes in the wars in the middle east? Does the term "collateral damage" excuse the killings, inadvertent as they may be? Only if we are accustomed to learning about and respecting the opinions of others at the grass roots level will we ever be able to reach meaningful compromises at the governing levels.

As a basis for really understanding how our government works or should work I would focus on our national vision and mission, and perhaps conclude the lesson with another exercise not unlike the one suggested above as a conclusion to our study of the Constitution. This one would have the student develop and write his or her understanding of what our mission and vision should be—for example, here is how I, were I a participant, might address the issues.

Today's Mission and Tomorrow's Vision
There is a Japanese proverb that says "Vision without action is a daydream. Action without vision is a nightmare."

Most individuals, most social organizations, most religious bodies, most universities and private secondary schools, and even most corporate entities have established missions and visions by which they regularly measure their effectiveness. With their mission statement they confirm to themselves and those they serve their purpose, accomplishments, and readily actionable objectives—the who, why, what and when of their daily actions. With their vision statement they disclose what goals they aim to reach and what image they would like to present in the future.

Regrettably, the United States of America does not have a clearly defined vision, understood by all of its citizens. We do not know where the path to a better world lies, nor what in essence it means to be an American. We have short-term goals dictated by the party in power in Washington, and a wonderful Constitutionally protected system of checks and balances to help guide our elected officials to achieve the urgent tasks at hand when called upon to do so. However, we postpone developing our vision of the future, setting aside the more important but not so urgent tasks as though there will always be plenty of time and another generation to accomplish them for us.

Unfortunately, this habit of taking the easy way stifles real long-range global thinking. We concentrate on the immediate problems: campaign finance reform, gun control, abortion rights, prescription drug programs, gay rights, etc.—but we are so bogged down in partisan politics that we can't even address these properly. And in the great scheme of things, were we to take no action on them, the world would continue on course, at least for the time being.

This is not to say that inaction is all right—every one of these immediate problems is important to American society and deserves our attention. But the larger share, or at least an equal share, of our attention should be on long-range global issues that affect mankind and human survival: nuclear disarmament, feeding and healing the world, and saving the environment. These should all be part of a clearly elucidated vision that strives for peace, prosperity, tolerance, and truth, at home and around the world. Such goals should be used by our elected officials and by each and every one of us to measure our actions every day. The vast majority of Americans would gladly trade some of our comforts and conveniences for a feeling of pride in being part of a country that is truly the world leader. And we can all participate in this collective responsibility.

America's Values?
Yes, we have our Declaration of Independence, our Constitution with its Bill of Rights, our Pledge of Allegiance, and our mottos "In God We Trust" and "E Pluribus Unum," as statements of national purpose. And we have every four years the platform drafted by the winning political party as a road map of sorts, to be fleshed out in the incumbent's State of the Union addresses, much of which is disregarded as the four-year term progresses.

But ask your friends and neighbors. Ask a stranger. Ask a teacher, a leader of industry, your clergyman, even your senator or representative, what does America stand for? What are those basic values that set us apart from every other nation that has ever existed, exists now, or ever will exist? I contend that you will get a multitude of answers, many of them even conflicting. It's understandable. Most of us are somewhat hazy on the basic premises underlying Thomas Jefferson's soaring words in the Declaration of Independence. Even the most conscientious among us have trouble remembering and enumerating the Articles of the Constitution and the Bill of Rights.

Do your elected representatives in Washington really support, or even remember, their party's platform in the last election, let alone remember or support what the president had to say in the State of the Union address? And as for The Pledge of Allegiance, we can't even agree on the applicability of its key phrase, "one nation under God." How about our motto "In God We Trust"? Some of us believe in God, but many do not believe in, let alone "trust," Him or Her.

So let us, for starters, propose a national vision statement that we can all rally around, drawing on the powerful messages that form the common core of our national history. Let's start by examining The Declaration of Independence and the Constitution of the United States of America.

Both documents have as their foundation what are called natural laws, a body of unchanging moral principles regarded as the basis for all human conduct, from which man-made laws and a political system must arise.

The well-known words of Jefferson's Declaration bear repeating here: "...that all Men are created equal, that they are endowed by their Creator with certain unalienable Rights, that among these are Life, Liberty, and the Pursuit of Happiness—That to secure these Rights, Governments are instituted among men, deriving their

just Powers from the Consent of the Governed...."[35] Our vision statement must encapsulate the essence of these immortal words when applied to our own citizens as well as to the citizens of other nations whom we hope to influence. All men are "created equal," but our citizens are not all "treated" as equal.

The same respect must be paid to the spirit of the Constitution. The delegates who wrote the Constitution held in highest regard the same Jeffersonian principles. Those same unalienable rights are central to the purpose of the Constitution which was "to form a more perfect Union, establish Justice, insure domestic Tranquility, provide for the common defence, promote the general Welfare, and secure the Blessings of Liberty to ourselves and our Posterity...."[36] The writers envisioned a central government strong enough to ensure those rights.

Still not entirely satisfied that they had anticipated every possible eventuality in the 1789 Articles of the Constitution, Congress came back a few months later to add 10 Amendments "in order to prevent misconstruction or abuse of its powers,"[37] and these were ratified in 1791. Known henceforth as the Bill of Rights, these amendments further expanded on the rights outlined in the Declaration. Some of those unalienable rights I would like to see incorporated in the values expressed or implied where applicable in our nation's Vision Statement for the 21st Century:

- Amendment I: Freedom of religion, freedom of speech, freedom of the press, the right to

assemble, and the right to petition government for redress of grievances without fear of retribution.
- Amendment IV: The right of the people to be secure in their persons, houses, papers, and effects, against unreasonable searches and seizures.
- Amendment V: No deprivation of life, liberty, or property, without due process of law, and no taking of private property for public use without just compensation.
- Amendment VI: The right to a speedy (frequently and shamefully denied or disregarded) and public trial by an impartial jury in all criminal prosecutions, the right to be confronted by one's accusers as distinct from hearsay testimony, and the right to a compulsory process to obtain witnesses in one's favor and to have assistance of counsel for defense.[37]

Two other amendments, added after the original Bill of Rights, should also be considered when drafting our national vision:
- Amendments XV, XIX: The right to vote regardless of race, color, or gender.[38]

By embracing these fundamental rights and obligations in our national vision, and firmly implanting them in the minds and hearts of every young man and woman during primary, secondary and post-secondary education, as well as while performing service in any national service program, we will have gone a long way toward protecting our values and ensuring our future prosperity, both moral and economic. And in this way, we will truly *become*—note that I did not say continue to be—the model to which all good citizens and nations aspire. Note also that I use the term "values," a word regularly cited by our elected officials and diplomats when we are urging others to emulate our example. Yet, lacking some clearly-stated mission or vision, I venture to say that, if you asked a dozen diplomats or elected officials to define our "values," you would not get anything close to a consensus.

Some may say that these values include democracy; less often, some might include capitalism. Neither, however, is required by a society genuinely shaped and directed by the Declaration of Independence and the Constitution. Rather, what is required, what comes through loud and clear, is the concept of freedom and liberty. As Ron Paul, the noted libertarian, former congressman and Presidential contender, succinctly put it, "Our country's founders cherished liberty, not democracy."

And, as we have advanced, and continue to advance, freedom in our nation, our vision should include exporting this idea of freedom around the globe. I would argue that this is our most important export.

I have focused primarily on our nation's vision, but the same exercise would apply to the development of a mission. The mission, however, might well change from one generation to the next, from one administration to the next, or even from one year to the next.

Students of our Civics lessons thinking along the above lines, should be able to effectively complete their exercise of developing sample national mission and vision statements. Perhaps the second most critical of the courses would be Media Literacy, and again the basics of this must be instilled as a foundation for voting.

Media Literacy

Young people across the country from middle school to college are unprepared to assess the information they encounter online, on cable news, or in any other local or national news source. Two leading researchers, Sam Wineburg and Sarah McGrew of the Stanford History Education Group, studied approximately 8000 students and concluded that, at every level, middle school, high school and college, there was a lack of preparation, and an inability to separate factual material from biased promotions.[39]

Many if not most of our students do not have access to a nationally recognized and respected newspaper such as the *Wall Street Journal* or *The New York Times* or, if they do, they do not have the time to read it nor the interest. But most if not all of them will undoubtedly have in their possession virtually at all times smart phones and/or other news gathering instruments, and will be accustomed to getting all their news in this fashion. It will typically come from Facebook, Twitter and other social media, and much of it will fall into the category of "fake news." This had become particularly prevalent during the final year of the Obama administration and during the Trump administration where the President himself was an avid user of Twitter. Much of the news distributed in this fashion is impulsive and backed up by little if any investigative reporting. Much of it is in fact "fake" and offered merely to elicit a specific reaction, typically a reaction supporting the rantings of the author, though there is also a fake news industry that is simply out to make money based on its advertising rates and the number of "hits" its shock news stories drive. Trump's advisor used the term "alternate facts" to describe the falsehoods emanating from their office. This would be amusing if it were not that they deemed the practice of spreading "alternate facts" as an acceptable form of communication.

Of course, the ultimate alternate fact would seem to be Trump's claim late on election day in 2020, and perpetuated by him thereafter, that he had actually won the election, when, in fact, the electoral college vote for Mr. Biden had already reached the 270 goal and was continuing to climb.

Here are some particularly egregious examples. The year 2015 was the hottest then on record. Then 2016 set a new record for the hottest year during which the month of July was the hottest month on record. Setting aside whether or not these temperatures were caused by human activities and carbon emissions, 45 percent of Republicans, according to a Gallup poll, simply don't believe these temperature facts.[40] Apparently they have been brainwashed by social media and believe only the side of social media that supports their position. However, I would have to believe that there are plenty of other social media postings supporting the correct temperature facts.

Unfortunately, many of us no longer respect the word of the experts. Not only would we rather take the word of a random posting on Facebook than that of the scientific community when considering the effects of climate change, we question overwhelming evidence and the opinions and advice of the medical profession concerning the safety of vaccines whether for measles, polio, COVID-19 or any other disease.

False claims posted on Facebook that have gone viral include a claim that the Pope had endorsed Donald Trump, a claim that Ireland was taking in from the United States refugees opposed to Trump, a multitude of ongoing false claims by Q-Anon the conspiracy theorists, and an endless ongoing trail of false claims by others, many of which are described below.

Myths
In an article addressing the 2020 Democratic presidential candidates, David Brooks compared the stories that then frontrunner Bernie Sanders told with the stories coming out of the mouth of President Trump. Mr. Brooks makes the point that they both rely on what he calls their "myths," Mr. Trump's being an old us versus them populist theory that "The coastal elites are greedy, stupid people who have mismanaged the

country, undermined our values and changed the face of our society." Trump followers "don't believe that myth, they inhabit it."[41] No matter how many lies he tells, no matter how corrupt and scandalous his behavior, if he stays within the myth, they stay within him. Mr. Sanders' myth, on the other hand, is another old us vs. them theory that "The corporate and Wall Street elites are rapacious monsters who hoard the nation's wealth and oppress working families."[41] Looked at through this lens, a primary opponent, Mike Bloomberg, was simply a billionaire who, when Mayor of New York, defended police targeting blacks and, when running for the Democratic nomination, used his wealth to buy power. Those who look at Mr. Bloomberg more objectively see "a successful entrepreneur who took his management skills into public service and then started giving his wealth away to reduce gun violence and climate change."[41]

A common myth posited by the liberal side of the media—note that I use the term "the liberal side of the media" rather than "the liberal media." The latter term as currently used implies to me that the entire media is liberal which as evidenced by Fox News, it is not— is that wages for typical workers and income for typical households have been stagnant for several decades. While labor has not shared in the gains in anything close to what capital has shared, its wages and income have not been stagnant. Michael Strain in his 2020 book *The American Dream Is Not Dead* gives a wealth of statistics showing that American workers do indeed enjoy the fruits of their labor, at least to a degree. Wage growth has far outpaced inflation by 20 percent to 40 percent over the approximately three decades ending in 2016, depending on the specific category of wage earners broken down by income percentile.[42] More recent data for the first eleven quarters of the Trump administration shows increases in wages for the bottom 10 percent of earners over age 25 averaged 5.9 percent annually, wages for the middle quartiles 3.2 percent and for the top 10 percent about 3 percent. For the less educated workers over 25, those without a high school degree, wages increased annually by 6.1%. For teens the figure is 5.8%, for 20 to 24-year-olds 4.4 percent and for 25 to 35-year-olds 4.8%.[43] More Americans are escaping poverty. In the most recent period for which statistics are available, 2016 to 2018, those earning less than $25,000 declined by 5%, and those making between $100,000 and $200,000 increased by 8%, promising figures for both the working class and the middle class.[43] These figures of course precede any negative trends caused by the COVID-19 pandemic.

Between the Trump administration and its followers and the liberal media, the interpretation of the effect of Mr. Trump's largest financial impact, that is up until the COVID 19 stimulus, centered around the $1.5 trillion 2017 tax cut. It was promoted by the administration to boost annual wages by $4000 per family, encourage investment, and foster ongoing economic growth. After implementation, the administration claimed that it in essence accomplished those goals. The liberal-sided media, on the other hand, reported wage growth as miniscule, and claimed that beneficiary corporations used the savings to finance a $1 trillion stock buyback rather than investing in new job producing plant and equipment.

Completely different stories—whom should we believe? That is for the reader to decide based on their evaluation of the news provider.

How to Evaluate a News Provider
Where should we get our news? When in this current environment can we believe that the news we obtain from a newspaper, magazine, cable news channel, TV or radio station or network, internet site or Facebook, is accurate and suitable not only for us to believe, but for us to pass on to our family, neighbors and community of friends? Paul Janensch in an opinion piece addressed five standards from the code of ethics of the Society of Professional Journalists:

Does the news provider value accuracy? Is being right more important than getting a scoop. Are quoted claims verified, facts checked?

Does the news provider act independently? Is the news presented for the benefit of the general public or to serve the interests of an individual seeking or holding an office or a political party or a social cause? Are the reports that are presented as facts, not as opinions or editorials, truly unbiased?

Does the news provider label opinion pieces, editorials and other commentary as such? We all want to hear commentary as well as factual reporting, but we also want to know when the news reported is indeed simply commentary.

Does the news provider identify sources? If a source is "anonymous," "unnamed," merely identified as "reliable," then it should always appear to the educated reader as questionable. Therefore, if the provider uses one of these terms, the reason for not naming the source should be clearly indicated, thereby giving the reader the best chance of determining the accuracy.

Does the news provider correct errors? Regardless of the above, even the best providers occasionally make errors. The enlightened reader accepts this as long as the errors are corrected on the air or in clear view.[44]

Does our free press encourage these five criteria? Under the Trump administration, the free press was being challenged as in no other time in history. Mr. Trump makes a habit of referring to the press as the harbinger of "fake news" when it publishes anything that might question the accuracy of his statements, his motives for them, or anything that might reflect negatively on his performance, past, present or future. Unfortunately, other leaders worldwide have adopted this same practice, admittedly not to the same extent, creating a global pandemic of fake news.

In response, the disease and its effect on the freedom of the press is exacerbated by some governments. Jordan, for example, has adopted a law punishing those who publish "false news." Journalists in Cameroon have been jailed for publishing fake news. Chad banned social media access for a year due to fake news. The cure for some can be worse than the disease.[45]

The independent free press around the globe is threatened by the rise of the internet as a news source of preference. Bombarded with falsehoods, It is increasingly difficult for one to know what to believe. Can democracies survive under this assault when governments and individuals cannot agree on a common set of facts? No easy answers, but hopefully, without compromising the freedom of the press, the internet companies can do a better job of patrolling the web and sorting out obviously misleading and/or malicious news. Congressional hearings on the issue are being held. And the press could do a better job of adhering to the five afore mentioned ethical criteria.[45]

Idea Laundering

"Idea Laundering" is a term in current use that was first used by Nick Confessore way back in 2003 in a *Washington Monthly* article describing some hedge funds' deceptive lobbying practices at the time. According to Alan Tonalson, a noted research fellow at the U.S. Business and Industry Council Educational Foundation, the term now encompasses a host of practices by "special interests (like corporations) using think tanks to issue materials that push the particular agendas of these funders while garbing them in quasi-academic raiment to create the impressions of objectivity and intellectual respectability. In other words, it's become practically standard operating procedure...for outfits with scholarly sounding names like 'The Brookings Institution' to put out reports and articles that flack for the companies and other donors ...that pay the rent without disclosing the hand that's feeding them." Mr. Tonalson says this practice can be overcome if the media, when quoting staffers from these organizations as experts on this or that issue, reveal the source of the tank's funding, as it may relate to the issue. He further states that the government could play a role. Local, state and federal legislatures should pass what he calls "Truth in Testifying Acts," so that, when hearing input from these think tanks, of which most of the major ones are located in Washington, they require them to disclose any of their funders who might have a financial interest in the issues being addressed. The public would then be in a better position to judge the credibility of the input, much of which is presented by the think tanks' staffers to whom they have assigned the impressive title of "scholar" or "fellow" as proof of their expertise.[46]

Other egregious example of idea laundering are those random and rambling thoughts conjured up by ideologues with no scientific basis to support them, typically the result of grievance studies perhaps initiated with good intent to examine and correct a legitimate grievance, but taken to such an extreme as to produce an irrational and ridiculous example of political correctness.

Peter Boghossian, in a Wall Street Journal opinion piece, "'Idea Laundering' in Academia," cites several examples including "fat shaming." Typically, these ideas start with so-called grievance studies, are picked up by an academic with a passionate opinion based on some imagined social injustice, for example, the negativity attached to obesity that makes obese persons feel bad about their condition and the thoughtless ridicule that often accompanies it, and regardless of the health issues involved, attempts to make obesity in every way a perfectly acceptable condition.

A paper is written, the writer gets colleagues on board, peers review the idea and a journal, in this case "Fat Studies," is born. A Board of Directors emerges, a pool of credentialed experts submits papers, articles are published, more ideas go in and there you have it—a new knowledge is created. Activist scholars grab on to the idea, and make sure the journal is disseminated to higher education via well-respected publishing houses. As Mr. Boghossian puts it, "before long...ideas, prejudice, opinion and moral impulses" have been "laundered into 'knowledge.'"

And then, the originating scholars use the articles to gain credentials, promotions and tenure in their academic institution. Courses and tests designed around this "knowledge" follow![47]

The End of Expertise
The growing pandemic of fake news or alternative facts with which we are constantly bombarded is, of course, exacerbated by the Internet, its Wikipedia tool, and Twitter, Facebook and other social media dumping grounds for collecting any and all information, factual or false, dumped on it by sources ranging from the ill-informed and ill-intentioned to the well informed and scholarly. This has enabled those whom we used to label as know-it-alls to claim knowledge about a subject or issue that they have not researched beyond a left click, and to obviate the need for an expert in the field to inform them. Our relationship with true expertise has changed. In the past, while we might not have disputed the facts presented by the expert on any given subject, our envy of those who knew something that we didn't often translated into a ridicule of the nerds, geeks, eggheads and other educated elites, effectively masking our envy and feeling of inadequacy. In recent years, however, this has taken a new and extremely dangerous twist whereby our feeling of inadequacy and our antipathy to the educated elite has grown to the point that we no longer accept a fact coming from an expert based on research and evidence as any better that our opinion based on the word of our friend who has some secret "in," the word of some biased partisan being interviewed on extreme right or left wing cable news, or worse still our gut feel based on our oh so wise common sense. Any information or news, no matter how well researched and documented, that doesn't confirm our bias is tossed aside as fake news. This is particularly

prevalent in political news, but also thrives in other fields, health care in particular. Now the experts are still there in all fields, but solicited for advise in only the most consequential circumstances. Tom Nichols, in his article "How America Lost faith in Expertise" in *Foreign Affairs* gives several examples, saying that most sane people go straight to the doctors, lawyers and engineers "if they break a bone, get arrested, or need to build a bridge" using the expert as a technician and established knowledge as a convenience. "Stitch this cut in my leg, but don't lecture me about my diet...Help me beat this tax problem, but don't remind me that I should have a will...Keep my country safe, but don't confuse me with details about national security trade-offs."[48]

The Trump administration built a dangerous history of disregarding the experts' opinions when they conflict with the desires of corporate America oil companies, energy companies, manufacturers and transporters who rely on cheap fossil fuels. Clean air and clean water regulations developed or expanded under the Obama administration have been decimated at the expense of national and global health. In one of the most recent cases, the White House rejected a plan to tighten regulations on PM 2.5 industrial soot emissions recommended by public health experts and EPA officials. This plan was in the works prior to the COVID-19 pandemic and became even more urgent based on the worsening effect of air pollution on those infected with the virus. The scientific research done by the EPA's experts indicated that PM 2.5 pollution contributes to tens of thousands of premature deaths annually, and that even a slight tightening of the regulation could save thousands of American lives.[49]

Then there are those who, because they are indeed educated and knowledgeable in general, or perhaps in one particular field, have the right to weigh in on fields where they have no particular knowledge and compete for authority with the experts in those fields. Mr. Nichols cites the anti-vaccine movement, which "gained its greatest reach among people such as the educated suburbanites in Marin County, outside San Francisco." Parents of the school children "had just enough education to believe that they could challenge established medical science, and they felt empowered to do so—even at the cost of the health of their own and everybody else's children."[48]

This is a dangerous example of what can happen when we lose faith in the wisdom of the experts and join with others as we succumb to theories of conspiracy to cover up our inadequate knowledge.

Conspiracy Theories
Perhaps the most insidious form of false news is the conspiracy theory whose disciples hold on to it with a vengeance regardless of the arguments and evidence disproving it. When one is simply too ill informed to look at the issue rationally, and especially when the theory can be used to advance one's cause, excuse one's

ignorance or cover up one's shortcomings, the theory re-mains firmly imbedded.

These have been going on for centuries. Perhaps the most well known historically is, unfortunately, still with us in one form or another today—the theories rooted in antisemitism—Jews poisoned wells, Jews are responsi-ble for killing Jesus, plotting to control the world, prop-agating communism, and so on, creating evils respon-sible for all sorts of social and economic problems, and thus becoming the major propaganda weapon used by Adolph Hitler in his quest to establish the Third Reich at the top of the world order. While he failed, his legacy unfortunately lives on and has shown signs of new life in the current rise of antisemitism throughout Europe and pockets of the United States where the Jews are blamed for the economic failings of autocratic govern-ments, and the corrupt and antisocial behavior of mal-content tribes.

There isn't a damaging major world event that doesn't give birth to conspiracy theories. The Sandy Hook school massacre didn't happen. It's a story dreamed up by the gun control lobby to further their cause. 9/11 was fostered by American right-wing extremists and/or by the Jewish lobby to start a war in the Middle East sup-porting Israel and destroying their Arab enemies. Then, too, the medical field is ripe with conspiracies. The FDA will not support eastern and natural remedies because of the lobbying of Big Pharma, while they promote the harmful measles vaccines for the same reason.

The current climate is particularly fertile for conspiracies, as we are consumed by the COVID-19 pandemic about which at the outset we had little knowledge—easy to fill in our knowledge gap though, a bioweapon developed by the Chinese would seem to suit our need, or, better still, our immune systems are being weakened by the emissions from a plethora of 5G networks being developed worldwide. Then again, were we in China, we would be hearing that the virus was brought to them by infected members of the U.S. military on assignment near the China Sea.

QAnon, a group known for spreading various theories about deep state conspiracies used to undermine the policies and actions of President Trump, is best known for their theory that the President's enemies, including many prominent Democrats, are pedophiles and devil worshipers who extract hormones from children's blood. As we all unfortunately found out, a man who read the related QAnon story about Hillary Clinton and John Podesta running a child sex ring in a Washington DC pizza restaurant went there and opened fire with an assault rifle.

Another QAnon theory states that "John F. Kennedy, Jr., who died in a plane crash in 1999, is alive and hiding in rural Pennsylvania, biding his time until he re-emerges to back Mr. Trump's re-election bid."[50]

QAnon also is among those who blame the pandemic on Bill Gates in his quest to use it to profit from an eventual vaccine, or even to gain control of the world's health system.[51]

Some conspiracy theories spring from a single grain of truth that gets expanded by the thought process to the effect that, if this is the case, isn't it possible that, or isn't it actually probable that—fill in the next step—is likely. I'm reminded of *Lab 257* written by Michael Christopher Carroll about the Plum Island Animal Disease Laboratory across the sound from Lyme, Connecticut, that in its early days was studying biological weapon. So far all correct, the location, and the purpose of the lab. But the theory espoused is that it is no coincidence that Lyme disease was the result of something gone awry just across the sound from Lyme, Connecticut, at the laboratory when it was studying biological weapons. After the book was published, we never heard much more about the theory. That seems rather strange. Of course then there were no social media avenues comparable to today's for the story to go viral.

When one is frustrated by having no knowledge on a given subject, or worse, a very limited knowledge, joining the conspiracy and convincing yourself that you are somewhat in control is comforting. President Trump was the master of this game. His claims that most of his negative press arose, not from his ignorance or incompetence, but from a deep state of his detractors supported by the liberal media, were a convenience that kept him in command. But his luck ran out when his claim of winning the 2020 election, followed by his claim that massive fraud in the election process perpetuated by that same deep state accounted for the vote count results, were proven to be completely unsubstantiated. His claims were a dangerous attack on our democracy, but, based on his previous habit of disregarding the truth, not unanticipated. Perhaps more concerning was the support for the President and his claims by most of the Republican senators and other Republican officials who clearly put their self-interests and the interests of their party ahead of those of the nation.

Slow Media

Of course, no one can tell what the next generation of social media will bring, just as no one could have anticipated television replacing radio, or the Internet replacing much of what we were used to getting from television. While the public is slowly losing some confidence in Facebook and Twitter as reliable news sources, we cannot count on them to do an about-face. They rely on sensationalism, deception and outrage to fuel their advertisers' tanks. Perhaps Google or Microsoft, or possibly some start up, will develop something more attuned to our needs. Whatever it is, it will undoubtedly address our desire for at least some degree of privacy and at least some degree of curation. Annalee Newitz in a *New York Times* opinion piece envisions a "form of digital communication that promotes consensus-building and civic debate, rather than divisiveness and conspiracy theories."[52] The emphasis would be on the ability to access only news that you wish to access rather than being bombarded with everything the media throws at you. You would have an expanded privacy setting filtering out useless and misleading information that you do not need nor desire. All sorts of apps would be available to help you sort through and select the news categories of interest, not merely to eliminate abusive or false information as some apps currently do. Newitz refers to a new type of news dissemination that is capable of this curation as "slow media" using a term from *Algorithms of Oppression* by Professor Safia Umoja Noble. New digital public places where we gather will closely mimic physical public places where we choose to congregate, town halls, concerts and other informative and friendly social gatherings. We will take back the responsibility for maintaining public space from the corporations presently designing and directing our social media.[52]

Confirmation Bias
Our course on how to separate fact from fiction would offer immeasurable benefits. The underlying theme of the course would be the absolute necessity of examining both sides of an issue before formulating an opinion. Read the opinions and editorials from both the conservative and liberal city or area newspapers. If you feel you have to view cable news, then watch both the conservative and liberal channels. Don't fall into the trap of "confirmation bias," i.e. reading and listening to only the side that typically corresponds with your ideology. Keep an open mind. Don't fall into the equally insidious trap of desirability bias, forming your opinion on what you want to hear and believe even in the face of contradicting evidence.

Ideally the cable news channels would adhere to a version of a "fairness doctrine" requiring them to present opposing views in addition to their own views on the issues. Better still, these different views could be addressed in debate form. Unfortunately, however, these news sources make their living catering to their own base.

Freedom of Speech and an End to Political Correctness

This course will help us understand how, once we have a better handle on what constitutes appropriate civil behavior, we can put an end to the political correctness nonsense that has so captivated us for the past few decades. Today, no one can say anything about someone's personal traits or beliefs, even in jest, without fear of not only hurting someone's feelings or insulting them, but of being politically, if not legally, punished for doing so. The first good example that I can remember offhand of how far this kind of super-sensitivity has gone was the political fallout occasioned by President Obama's innocent remark about Kamala Harris back when she was California Attorney General long before her campaign for higher office when we all got to know her better. Introducing her at a Democratic fundraiser, he described his friend as "brilliant...dedicated...tough," but then added that "she also happens to be, by far, the best-looking attorney general in the country."[53] Can we imagine anyone taking offense, or even recalling a comment of that nature, a few administrations ago? There would have been a few smiles and perhaps a few chuckles, probably followed by "You're not so bad for a president yourself, Mr. Obama." Isn't it possible that the President's opponents had more significant issues with his governance about which to complain?

Avoidance of political correctness, though the subject of a short course in itself, also will be a guideline for our other training course discussions. We will "tell it like it is" regardless of how disconcerting, even offensive, some of the issues may be to particular persons or groups. Unfortunately, on the campuses of our most revered colleges and universities, where freedom of speech should be paramount, we have taken the absurd steps, in order to avoid offending any student, discomforting them or hurting their feelings, of providing "safe spaces" on campus where they can avoid social contact with those of opposing opinions. These safe spaces represent the absolute opposite of what should be done because they erase even the opportunity for the students to discuss issues with those with opposing opinions who perhaps come from different backgrounds. We provide "trigger warnings" on assigned literature that might include references to subjects, sexual, political, religious, etc. that might conflict with their upbringing and convictions.

Some of our institutions no longer extend invitations to controversial speakers, and, if they do and protests greet the announcement, they may be driven to disinvite them on the grounds that some students just can't cope. Greg Lukianoff, president and CEO, and Adam Goldstein, senior research counsel for the Foundation for

Individual Rights in Education, in their Wall Street Journal article "Law Alone Can't Protect Free Speech," cited Princeton's investigation of a professor because he wrote an op-ed disagreeing with activist demands—the public calling for Auburn University to fire a professor for expressing antipolice views online—and the hounding to suicide of a conservative North Carolina-Wilmington professor for abrasive public statements—all of this taking place within a space of just two weeks in the summer of 2020.[54]

Practically anything controversial can now be construed as a microaggression (a term most of us older graduates never even heard of).

Cancel Culture
This intolerance for discussing issues and ideas outside of the mainstream has of course taken on a whole new life in the aftermath of the Black Lives Matter protests. The "woke" culture committed to social justice, specifically racial justice, to which we all to some extent embrace, oversteps its bounds when it attempts to erase history and becomes a "cancel culture" by destroying monuments that offend certain races or ethnicities. We condemn other states or non-state actors, e.g. ISIS or Al Qaeda, when they destroy, and erase reference to, historical monuments commemorating figures from past cultures with whom they disagree. Yet many of us are destroying, or are in favor of those destroying, statues of Confederate generals for obvious reasons of defending slavery, statues of founding

fathers because of their part in supporting slavery, or statues of Christopher Columbus for his treatment of native Americans. Rather than destroying these relics and cancelling history, they should be moved to a park or other historical museum venue accompanied by text describing their historical significance, both the good and the bad.

Before, during and after the 2020 Black Lives Matter protests, professors, others in academia, and journalists, not fully aspiring to the woke culture were being condemned, censored and in some cases dismissed from their duties based on what they wrote or discussed.

Take the case of Harvard Professor Steven Pinker, who has suffered from the pen of the "speech police." For his oft-stated opinions that other factors may be at the heart of some of the injustices frequently attributed to racism, he was denounced by 550 academics who signed a letter demanding his removal (subsequently denied, fortunately) "from the list of 'distinguished fellows' of the Linguistic Society of America"—the cause of the demand, tweets and comments from years past suggesting that the high number of police shootings of Black people may not be the result of racism in the police force but rather of police having "disproportionately high numbers of encounters with Black residents," the problem therefore "not race, but too many police shootings." Professor Pinker's detractors also decried his use of the terms "urban crime" and "urban violence" as racially motivated "dog whistles," although the terms are widely used in sociology and law to describe exactly what they imply.[55]

Professor Pinker's position on nature versus nurture as a predictor of human behavior, opining that "characteristics like psychological traits and intelligence are to some degree heritable" has proven to be at odds with his politically correct critics. He also has shared former Harvard President Lawrence Summers' speculation that differences between the genders might account for women having less success in science and math careers, a speculation unpopular with his liberal colleagues that in part led to Mr. Summers' resignation from Harvard.[55]

While common sense would indicate to most of us that there are indeed certain character differences between the sexes, be they physical or hormonal for example, that are inherited, it has become forbidden to talk about them or even think about them.[55]

Then there is the case of Nathaniel Hiers, a math professor at the University of North Texas who was relieved from his position for criticizing the entire concept of "microaggressions" arguing that it "inevitably 'hurts diversity and tolerance' by encouraging people to see the worst in others."[56]

I sincerely hope that under influence of the Trump administration and others to follow, this approach to educating our youth that relies on political correctness will, to use a Trump phrase, "stop right now." We must be careful, though. Political correctness can, at times be a little tricky to ascertain. I leave it to the reader to determine whether President Obama's avoidance of terms like "radical Islamist terrorism" for fear of offending the vast majority of peace-loving Islamists around the world was correct. Or was Donald Trump on target when he used "radical Islamist terrorism" when he spoke of the threats coming from ISIS or any of the other radical groups with terrorist cells in the Middle East? They carry religious flags and shout Koranic verse when they attack, but are they really the face of Islam?

Religion

This course probably will be the most difficult of all to get into a national program and/or the education core, what with First Amendment concerns, but it is an extremely important course, if one of the purposes of the program is to give us all a better understanding of those from diverse backgrounds.

This should be a very broad overview with sections on the basic tenets of the major eastern and western religions written by scholars recognized for their expertise. The overarching message here should be that all religions rely on the observer's faith as taught by family and church, in addition to, or perhaps in place of, some limited historical evidence. We should address issues that demonstrate this, for example evolution versus creation, and we should focus on the controversy over the existence of God or a God, and what kind of God.

One could readily make a case for this lesson being globally the most important of all. Somewhere, sometime the whole world must learn this lesson if organized religion is to cease being the underlying cause of so many national and global wars. We must stop hating those of faiths other than ours, be they Jews, Christians, Muslims or others, for no other reason than worshipping another God who typically has nothing to do with our own daily lives. What better opportunity to foster mutual understanding and acceptance than during our early schooling—surely a better opportunity than now exists in many of our churches.

In his book *21 Lessons for the 21st Century*, Yuval Harari asks the question "Does God exist?" and answers "That depends on which God you have in mind: the cosmic mystery, or the worldly lawgiver?" The former, the cosmic mystery, he describes as "a grand and awesome enigma about which we know absolutely nothing" and which we invoke "to explain the deepest riddles of the cosmos. Why is there something rather than nothing? What shaped the fundamental laws of physics?"

The latter, the worldly lawgiver, on the other hand, we claim to know only too much about, for example what he "thinks about fashion, food, sex and politics," based on which, we "justify a million regulations, decrees, and conflicts." He tells some of us what we can and cannot, should or should not, think or do." This is the God of the faithful servants of a beneficent God, but also the "God of Crusaders and jihadists, of the inquisitors, misogynists, and homophobes." [57]

Another question to be addressed in this course is can the faithful including those identifying as evangelicals serve two master, God and country—country as identified for example by the mission and vision addressed in the civics lesson? Yuval Harari would lead me to think "yes," seeing the laws of Judaism, Christianity or Hinduism for example that were "very helpful in establishing and maintaining the social order for thousands of years" as "not fundamentally different from the laws of secular states and institutions." [57]

All of us ask what is the meaning of life, more specifically, what is the meaning of my life. What should I do in life. I think this can be broadly addressed in our course on religion without leading to specific conclusions, but, rather leading our students to life long questioning. Without some background, we flounder. Most of us need a foundation, traditionally built for us by our forebears and parents. However, most, if not all, of us also benefit from overarching goals backed up by the vision of our country. This can be supported by the teachings of the above beneficent worldly God, but, unfortunately, as human history has taught us, derailed by other worldly Gods.

Harari, after considering both fiction and fact connected with the stories of life as transcribed in historical, philosophical and religious doctrine throughout the ages, concludes that the question which we should address is not "what is the meaning of life," but rather "how do we stop suffering."[58] These words to me make a compelling statement that, while we focus on the positive aspects of human achievement, we must also focus on the negative consequences— the magnificence of the pyramids and also the toll of human labor involved, the glory of Rome, and also the brutal punishment of those who opposed the emperors, the victories of the Russians on the eastern front and the raising of their red flags over Berlin, but also the cost of millions of German and Russian soldiers killed in the battles, the victory over terrorism in the Middle East at the expense of millions of civilians displaced or killed. Again, these are discussion points for this course, designed only to get our students thinking with an open mind.

Current Affairs

Current affairs should be taught at all levels of education, but how they are taught would of course be significantly different depending on the age and progress of the student. For example, in kindergarten and elementary school, the subject matter would only be briefly identified during class time. Then written pamphlets, typically known in the past as "Weekly Readers" would be handed out for reading at home and discussion with parents, the parents having been encouraged by the local education boards to get involved, at least to this extent, with their children's schooling. Brief discussions, probably followed by written tests in the middle and upper classes, would be given weekly, but the results would not be factored into the students' grades.

Parents throughout the grades stay involved! Tell your children what you think about the issues, but encourage them to think for themselves, and develop their own opinions. I'm reminded of a comment by Matthew Hennessey, Wall Street Journal opinion editor, that "The only thing worse than a teenage eye roll is a teenage parrot."[59] For the secondary education classes, it would be a good idea for our students to hear from "the experts," on both sides where applicable, of each of the major current issues of the times. For example, were the classes in place now, the issues covered might include the case for and against a single payer universal health care system, and gun control/safety as well as all the other issues that will be addressed in Chapter Nine where we discuss opportunities for political compromise.

Foreign Policy and Lessons in International Understanding

Here we would focus on how best to recover our reputation and be a world role model. George W. Bush had much to say about this in his 1999 memoir, *A Charge to Keep*, written when he was still governor of Texas: "The world seeks America's leadership, looks for leadership from a country whose values are freedom and justice and equality. Ours should not be the paternalistic leadership of an arrogant big brother, but the inviting and welcome leadership of a great and noble nation. We have a collective responsibility as citizens of the greatest and freest nation in the world. America must not retreat within its borders. Our greatest export is freedom, and we have a moral obligation to champion it throughout the world."[60]

In the run-up to the 2000 presidential campaign, he cautioned "Let us not dominate others with our power.... Let us have an American foreign policy that reflects American character. The modesty of true strength. The humility of true greatness. This is the strong heart of America."[61]

Though freedom may have a slightly different meaning to each of us, safe to say that most of us find its elements set forth unambiguously in our Bill of Rights. But for some it is not always a black and white issue regardless of the rhetoric of our political ideologues. And securing it to the satisfaction and benefit of all is never easy. Just consider that, while available evidence tells us that wearing a mask during the COVID-19 pandemic enhances our safety and the safety of others, some are of the absurd perception that it infringes on their freedom and their rights.

The difference between exporting freedom and exporting democracy should be addressed during this course as it is a key issue regarding our foreign policy. Many societies are generations away from democracy. Look at our failed attempts to bring real democracy to Iraq and Afghanistan. Consider how all the brave promises of the Arab Spring, the democratic uprisings that originated in 2010 in Tunisia and quickly took hold in Egypt, Libya, Syria, Yemen, Bahrain, Saudi Arabia, and Jordan, have to date, with the possible exception of Tunisia, failed to bear fruit for any of those nations, leaving several of them worse off than before. However, this is not the end of the story. A measure of freedom is within the reach of some of these nation-states that are still under clerical and other non-democratic governments. They can still find their own evolutionary path at their own sustainable pace. Others, like Syria, are so totally in the grip of oppression—the Assad regime, the Islamic State (ISIS)—to need outside assistance to break free. Saudi Arabia and Iran must learn to share control of the region and foster a cooperative effort that will benefit all. While we're making progress encouraging the Arab states to join forces with each other and with Israel in order to present a more formidable deterrent to Iran, it is abundantly clear that we can't do much more to foster this cooperative effort.

Beyond our embrace of the concepts of freedom here and around the globe, and democracy here and where possible, this foreign policy lesson must look at the other global issues for which Americans feel responsible. These would include combatting climate change, and also, as described in George W. Bush's 2006 State of the Union address, taking "the offensive by encouraging economic progress and fighting disease and spreading hope in hopeless lands. Isolation would not only tie our hands in fighting enemies, it would keep us from helping our friends in desperate need. We show compassion abroad because Americans believe in the God-given dignity and worth of a villager with HIV/AIDS or an infant with malaria or a refugee fleeing genocide or a young girl sold into slavery."[62]

And even as we pursue these admirable goals, we must also maintain as part of our mission the ability to field a strong, capable, modern military force that is trained to win, and ready when military action is in our vital national interest. George W. Bush's socalled Bush Doctrine called for pre-emptive unprovoked action by the United States against emerging threats—action that could include military attack, promoting regime change, and other tactics and strategies to protect our interests. This doctrine was intended to encourage our adversaries to pursue diplomacy before exposing themselves to military attack.[63]

During the ensuing Obama years we were still in the infancy of dealing with growing worldwide terror organizations and, due in part to the mixture of friends and enemies battling in Iraq and Syria, and our antipathy to both the Assad regime in Syria and the radical Islamic section of the militants opposing him, we did not develop a comprehensive diplomatic and military strategy for defeating these adversaries. The Trump administration appeared to see the urgency and dangers of an ideological war being waged by radical Islam against our western values, and was committed to eliminating the Islamic State's capacity to make war, and the rogue elements of Iran and its proxy states. In line with the Bush doctrine, they followed through with this by their elimination of Iran's key military leader

General Soleimani and the ISIS leader Abu Bakr al-Baghdadi.

Our foreign policy should give our friends and enemies around the globe a picture of who we truly are and what they can expect from us whenever challenges and crises come our way. And by having our allies and our adversaries know us better, a less vulnerable, more secure world may become a reality.

Our students should have a basic grasp of the above in order to appreciate the specific foreign policy issues of the time—for example, they would need now to understand our involvement in the politics and conflicts in the Middle East and the real cost of their oil when we factor in the wars and our unwavering support of Israel. Our students must have a thorough understanding of our major foreign policy issues, not only to become better informed about our global leadership role, but also because they could well find themselves physically involved in them, either as part of our military force, or as humanitarian corpsmen serving in these areas as participants in a humanitarian aid or foreign service program. Similarly, our students need some knowledge of the foreign defense treaties into which we have entered, and of the depth of our commitments when the countries with whom we are aligned are threatened or invaded.

What is the difference between our obligations to NATO nations and Japan, and our obligations to Afghanistan and Ukraine, for example? When, according to our foreign and military policies, are "boots on the ground" justified? Under what circumstances should we deploy drone attacks? What are the legal and ethical differences between the treatment of prisoners captured from the military forces of a recognized state and those captured from non-statesponsored insurgent groups like Al Qaeda and ISIS?

The foreign policy curriculum could include a very basic discussion of the cultural differences between the secular and religious states of the world, the developed and non-developed, the poor and the wealthy, and the Sunnis and Shiites within the Muslim world. Why do Americans barely react, when some angry foreign activists burn our flag, while the people of some other nations respond to almost any disrespect of their cultural icons, real or perceived, with violence in the streets, suicide bombings, and civilian beheadings? Why are we often so unsuccessful in negotiating with their leaders? Well, quite possibly, it is simply because we fail to recognize that the fundamental beliefs that drive their priorities and ours are different.

We have so much going for us—so much freedom of choice, so much confidence in the rightness of our system of government—that we fail to recognize how constrained others' lives are. The burning of our flag or the anti-American raving of some fanatic Muslim cleric, is not as demanding of our attention as who wins the Super Bowl, what restaurant we'll visit tonight, what crime story has captured the news. How can we relate to a foreign culture in which the common man can never afford to attend lavish sporting events, knows no religious freedom, and has virtually all his beliefs and behaviors prescribed by custom? For this isolated individual, any offense against his or her country's sanctity and traditions, including the burning of the Koran or the ridiculing of some ayatollah by people in some far-off land, becomes a major incident.

At times during the war in Afghanistan, we experienced a troubled phenomenon among the Afghan troops who were supposed to be our allies. Repeatedly, one or two of them broke ranks during a joint mission to turn on us, wounded or killed American "comrades" in their company. The attacks were made most often by Afghans from isolated rural areas, where their entire life experience up to the time they become soldiers is of their villages' religious and social codes, scarcely modified over the centuries. Though the rogue soldiers were often taken for Taliban fighters, Afghan advisers insisted the men were driven by personal anger and the perception that their country's sanctity was disrespected by the free-wheeling Americans. In this way their acts were demonstrations of respect for their beliefs, not of political insurgency. While we should in no way excuse or condone these actions, nor accept any blame for them, this lesson in international understanding as I have labeled it could sensitize our young people to the exceptional part played by religious beliefs in orthodox Muslim societies, the better to avoid behaviors and remarks seen as disrespectful.

Immigration

This lesson will be an extremely important and welcome part of our curriculum, especially since so many of our students will be the children of immigrants, or, in many cases immigrants themselves.

Our country, more than any other on the globe, was built in great part by immigrants, and continues to benefit by a constant flow of immigrants, skilled and unskilled. Approximately 14 percent of us, including Elon Musk, CEO of Tesla and developer of several notable high-tech companies, are immigrants. Others like Steve Jobs, co-founder and former CEO and Chairman of Apple, had an immigrant parent. During the Trump administration, the role of immigration in our progress, was being examined more closely than ever in the past. Fortunately, the Biden administration has reversed this trend and no longer bars immigrants based solely on their Islamic religion or their origin from a country that provides haven for terrorists. Hopefully we will examine and, if necessary, improve our vetting process to the satisfaction of all, bearing in mind, however, that the existing process is already very extensive. A course in our program explaining all of this, if properly developed, should foster improved relations and good will among those starting off with opposing views by clearly describing the benefits of a larger workforce to the sustained growth of our economy, the addition of highly educated engineers, scientists and physicians to our society and economy, and the tradition and values associated with aiding political refugees and those escaping economic misery. We should be able to absorb those in desperate need escaping from Afghanistan or attempting to cross our southern border.

How can America at whose doorway stands the Statue of Liberty welcoming the tired, the poor and the "huddled masses yearning to breathe free" continue to build impediments to immigration based primarily on unfounded fears of increased criminal activity and loss of job opportunities for those of us already on board? "The dominant American view until the late 20th century was that 'we welcome all kinds of people but we expect them to assimilate into some range of standard values, behaviors, aspirations, ambitions.'" We need to get back to that view, realizing that, while the immigrant stream is perhaps more diverse than ever, we have "never been an ethnic state or a hodgepodge of groups, but a 'national community' that stands for a distinctive creed still worth aspiring to."[64]

Not only does this thinking foster a national community of values reflecting proper concern for the well-being of all Americans regardless of birth, background, and social and economic standing, but, by keeping our doors open to deserving and needy immigrants, it, as has been proven, enhances our economic growth and the resultant improvement in the standard of living for all. Also, since Americans are having fewer children, we need more, not less, immigration to produce the goods and services to provide the necessary growth. As Neel Kashkari noted in his

New York Times article, "Immigration Is Practically a Free Lunch for America."[65]

Climate Change and Environmental Protection

If you believe as I do that climate change poses a threat to our future comparable to nuclear war or an apocalyptic global pandemic, then learning this lesson and supporting and taking action to counter it, is surely one of the most critical steps to becoming a good American and a good citizen of the world. Here all of us individually can take steps to combat this threat, and make these steps part of our daily habits. And collectively we can follow the advice of Bill McKibben who, in his book *Falter,* recommends community organizing and nonviolent demonstrating to help prevent worst case scenarios that he claims include the "death of all ocean life by 2100" and "a 21 percent drop in human cognitive abilities, also by 2100."[66]

We're all aware that there are many factors that go into protecting our future and the future of the planet. Of the most critical it would seem are nuclear disarmament in order to eliminate the threat of nuclear war, and an international approach to preparedness for pandemics to include the maintenance of disease laboratories of continuing research, adequate worldwide stockpiles of personal protective equipment and testing supplies, and adequate hospitalization and testing capacity. Nuclear disarmament and pandemic preparedness both require collective action fostered by bipartisan agreement. But the one area where we can all participate individually and make a difference is in the protection of the planet, both by combating climate change by reducing our carbon footprint, and by minimizing and controlling waste and disposal for the sake of cleaner air and water.

Now, in Chapter Nine, I address the controversial aspects of climate change, both man's contribution to the problem as well as the cost to the economy of combatting it. Regardless of one's position on the extent of our contribution and the lengths we should go to in combatting climate change, there is a compelling case for agreement that we, especially the United States, historically the largest emitter of pollutants, are at least partially responsible. And climate change or no, there are huge health gains in cleaning up our air and water, even if we elect to do nothing about the increase in droughts, wildfires, and floods brought about by climate change regardless of man's involvement.

Our collective ability for positive change, started and well underway during the Obama administration, has unfortunately been thwarted by the Trump administration's decision to pull out of the Paris Accord and to revoke or roll back approximately 100 regulations and "rules aimed at increasing fuel efficiency of cars and trucks;...limiting emissions of methane, a powerful greenhouse gas, from oil and gas wells; ...increasing the energy efficiency of appliances;" and even more egregious, discontinuing the Clean Power Plan."[67] Fortunately, however, California, New York and other states are taking matters into their own hands implementing restrictions tighter than those of the federal government, and President Biden has rejoined the Paris Accord.

The conventional wisdom now, as put forth by many experts including James Baker, George Schultz and Ted Halstead in their *Foreign Affairs* article "The Strategic Case for U.S. Climate Leadership" calls for encouraging the reduction of carbon emissions by an economy-wide and revenue-neutral carbon fee paid by emitters on emissions from stationary sources. The revenue would be returned directly to the American people in the form of a carbon dividend. The incentives to industry would replace, and be more effective than, much of the regulation currently imposed. Other nations would be similarly incentivized to reduce emissions when we impose on them a carbon tariff similar to our domestic fee, returnable again to the American people, on energy intensive imports. China, India and other foreign emitters would get on board and find it in their best interests to apply similar carbon fees on their emissions.[68]

There is a broad coalition including "19 Fortune 100 companies, three leading environmental nongovernmental organizations... five of the seven oil and gas supermajors, the largest solar company in the United States and three of the nation's leading utilities" working together on a plan for bipartisan action in Congress. The framework for the plan has been "endorsed by over 3500 U.S. economists, including the past four chairs of the Federal Reserve, 27 Nobel laureates, and 15 former chairs of the President's Council of Economic Advisors, including all eight former Republican chairs."[68]

Until the plan is implemented, there are actions that we as individuals can take if we are well informed regarding the cause and effects of climate change, wasteful consumption and improper disposal of nondegradable and toxic substances.

Becoming informed and taking action is absolutely critical to the development of good citizens. And it all starts with early childhood training, through primary and secondary education and throughout life. A good reference for these lessons would be *Drawdown—The Most Comprehensive Plan Ever Proposed to Reverse Global Warming* edited by Paul Hawken noted author, environmentalist and Executive Director of Project Drawdown. Sections of this publication could comprise a primer for elementary education purposes as well as a textbook for older students partaking in the series of lessons. It addresses "the 100 most substantive solutions to reverse global warming, based on meticulous research by leading scientists and policymakers around the world."[69]

Many of the solutions are, of course, related to clean energy, solar, wind, hydroelectric, etc., and even these are somewhat under our control as consumers. We can install energy-saving insulated windows, wall panels and roofing, and solar panels and/or heat pumps for heating and cooling. "Residential thermostats control 9 percent of US energy consumption" and the new smart thermostats can memorize your routines and preferences and help "reduce consumption at times of peak energy use, peak prices and peak emissions."[70] We can install

LED bulbs and lighting in our homes, and eventually will have to, as incandescent and fluorescent bulbs are phased out for energy saving purposes. LED uses only 10 percent of the energy to produce the same amount of light as incandescent and 50 percent of the energy that fluorescent lighting requires. Lighting accounts for 15 percent of global electricity, so we can make a significant difference by changing our habits.[71]

The other basic requirement, in addition to energy, in order to run a functioning household, at least in the developed world, is, of course, water. This likewise is not in sustainable endless supply, and we can individually make a difference in our consumption habits. Processing and transporting our water to point of use, whether from a municipal source or a private well consumes energy. The less we use showering, flushing toilets and cleaning, the less energy required. The less we heat the water for bathing and other purposes, the less energy is used. Most of the conservation under our control is simply a matter of being mindful every time we turn on a faucet. Then again, there are specific one time household actions that we can take, the most effective being installing low flush toilets which can reduce household water use by 19 percent.[72]

Many other solutions are well under the control of all of us. Take food for example. Harvard Professor Michael Pollan is quoted in *Drawdown* posing for argument the question "why bother" as it relates to steps we can take to protect the environment. Why bother when every little step I take is probably cancelled out by some non-caring individual somewhere who doesn't give a damn about protecting the planet and lives a lifestyle demonstrating that. One answer, albeit for the most ambitious of us, lies in reducing our carbon footprint by planting a garden and enjoying its fruits along with the lifelong reward of turning one's thoughts into action, of developing a relationship with the wonders of our natural world, and giving us a constant reminder that we can indeed make a difference.[73]

Home gardener or not, we can all join the homeowners using a new generation of energy saving, carbon reduction, clean cookstoves to cook our food. As of 2015, some 28 million of these stoves were in use worldwide, with a goal of 100 million by 2020 and universal adoption a decade later.[74]

The environmental costs of commercially growing and transporting our food are lowered proportionately by reducing the amount of food production required if we reduce food waste, both before and after it reaches us, but also by all of us in the developed world being more diligent in our buying habits, in meal planning, in using perfectly good products with an expired "use by" date. Simply stretching leftovers is another very effective way for us to reduce our carbon footprint.

But of course, as we are all constantly reminded, the most significant way that we as individuals in our eating habits can reduce our carbon footprint is by eliminating or reducing our consumption of meat products. Energy consumption related to grazing practices, the production of meat products, and the greenhouse gas emissions from cows and other livestock are estimated conservatively at 15 percent of global greenhouse gas emissions or even as much as 50% if all indirect emissions are included. I'm not suggesting this, but if all of us adopted a vegan diet eliminating all meat and dairy products, the emissions could be reduced by as much as 70 percent or by as much as 63 percent by only switching to a vegetarian diet allowing dairy products.[75] It's easy to see that even minor reductions in the consumption of meat products can make a significant difference.

The impact that we have on our environment is a function of not only consumption habits, considering both quantity and technology used in producing food and other consumer goods, but also of course, by the size of our population responsible for the consumption. So, in addition to addressing our consumption habits, it has proven to be well within our power to control the population size by family planning, i.e. giving women the option of having "children by choice rather than chance." Examples include Iran where in the 1990s fertility rates were halved simply by involving the clerics, educating the public and providing free access to contraceptives. In Bangladesh average family birth rates were reduced from six in the 1980s to two thirty years later using female health workers providing door to door care for women. Here again, while the message must be spread by the government agencies and clerics, success is the result of our individual actions. But, when we talk about what we can all individually do, this particular lesson of course can't be addressed in the early stages of education, but must be addressed before family planning becomes an urgent issue to be dealt with.

Our transportation habits too make a large contribution to our carbon footprint. Transport emissions of carbon dioxide are second only to electricity generation emissions. We have all seen the statistics related to the carbon emissions from air travel, but let's look at our daily transportation habits. Using mass transit when and where available instead of our personal automobiles for commuting offers a real opportunity for us to individually reduce emissions, and many of us are aware of this and attempt to do so. Some of us are also switching from gasoline and diesel powered vehicles to electric vehicles, and more of us will do likewise in the future as more models become economical and switching stations more available. The more efficient electric engines, 60 percent efficient as opposed to 15 percent for gasoline powered, reduce carbon dioxide emissions by 50%.[76] Of course, balanced against that are the additions to the carbon footprint from the generation and transportation of electricity to the charging stations.

And, were we more like some others around the globe, we would completely eliminate much of our local automobile travel by switching to bicycles, either pedal powered or electric. In Denmark, for example, 18 percent of local trips are made by bicycle, in the Netherlands

27 percent, but in our car-crazy United States only 1 percent. Increasing our bicycle use will require municipalities to address bike lanes and paths and other infrastructure improvements.[77]

We have mentioned above the detrimental effects of waste, as it relates to our food consumption. But discarded food is only a small part of the consumption that we waste. We have become a throw away society. It was not much more than a generation ago that we, our mothers to be specific, darned our socks and reversed the worn collars on our dress shirts. Adult clothing, men's and women's, was used for many years, frequently with stitched repairs. Virtually all children's clothes and sporting goods, unless severely worn out, were handed down to younger siblings. Broken furniture and toys were more frequently repaired than discarded. I grew up with fine porcelain dinner plates that had been in the family for generations that had been repaired with staples!

Now, perfectly good clothing goes to Goodwill Industries or other second hand shops, after very little use because the owner is simply "tired of wearing it" or it has gone out of fashion. Much of it even ends up in the landfill. Fortunately, among the latest generation now out on their own, there is a growing contingent who sees the error in this lifestyle, wears clothing throughout its useful life and even utilizes these secondhand shops as their clothiers. I wouldn't expect that we'll get back to stapling our broken dinner plates, but I would expect that there will be a resurgence of interest in antique furniture and other antique household items and supplies and the shops providing them. Beauty and fine art should not go out of style simply from the passing of time.

On the brighter side, roughly half of our household waste that no longer has a use and that was traditionally disposed of in the town dump or regional landfill can now be recycled, specifically paper, plastic, metal, and glass. In most communities, we now have the service available, and we can all do our part. While there is energy required to recycle, when the land, air and water pollution option of the landfill is considered, this is a favorable tradeoff. And "producing new product from recovered materials often saves energy."[78]

Economic Theories

Since the 2008 financial crisis, economics has a new relevance for all of us. Unfortunately, in only 23 states are high schools required to offer an introduction to economic theory and in only 17 states are students required to take an economics course.[79] Therefore, many of our high school graduates will have had little schooling in this subject. So what material should be included in this course?

In the 2020 Democratic presidential primaries, Vermont's self-declared Socialist Senator Bernie Sanders gained a widespread following from the youth element, the majority of whom when asked what form of government they prefer chose socialism over capitalism. Now therefore, it is quite apparent that we need to provide an adequate foundation on which one can stake or deny this claim. It is easy to see why so many claim a preference for socialism over capitalism. The socialism that they see is the form of government that exists in the Scandinavian countries where the high taxes paid by everyone are accepted because they support generous welfare with an effective safety net, health care for all, and high quality education for all regardless of the economy of their local community. Everyone benefits. Polls continually give Scandinavia and particularly Denmark the highest ratings for life satisfaction. Taxes under capitalism, according to our youth element, are not paid effectively by everyone, but are structured to benefit the upper and upper middle classes at the expense of the lower and lower middle classes. The owners and upper management of corporations, the pharmaceutical industry, the arms traffickers, and those who financially support our elected officials profit with a high standard of living while the working man struggles to put food on the table, pay for his health care and afford his family a suitable education. Well, one might say with some justification that we have appropriately compared the Scandinavian countries with the United States, but we have not compared socialism with capitalism, and the correct comparison must be taught as part of our lessons in living. Both Scandinavia and the United States operate under a capitalist economic system characterized by the means of production and distribution residing in the hands of private individuals or privately owned corporations with wages and prices determined by the market. The difference is in how the profits are taxed and distributed. In a socialist system, the means of production and distribution are in the hands of the state where wages and prices are determined by the government. Even the self-proclaimed socialist Bernie Sanders was not promoting this; he is more aptly described as a social democrat, not as a true socialist.

As we teach the above lessons, we should clarify that socialism is not always the Scandinavian model that some of us desire but is more typically represented by the autocracy and poverty of Cuba, Nicaragua, Russia and Venezuela. The Scandinavian model is really capitalism similar to ours but with appropriate regulations to ensure an adequate standard of living and quality of life for all.

In our lessons, students will be exposed to the basic economic theories that drive our society and others. Economist Donald Marron shows that it can be done quite simply in his brief book, *30 Second Economics,* which would be excellent for the recommended reading list at the conclusion of this course on economic theories. Marron quickly runs through the essentials of such concepts as supply and demand, gross national product, socialism, property rights, and the ideas of some of the most influential thinkers in the field. It would not take long, for example, to introduce the student to the basic *laissez faire* tenets of the Scot moral philosopher and free market champion Adam Smith's "invisible hand" and

Milton Friedman's free market capitalism, or the government intervention-guided theories of John Maynard Keynes and his modern day advocate Paul Krugman. Our course could be very simple, with written material, and/or a lecture or two, presented in a form that everyone can follow and understand. Here's how I would do it...

Start by explaining that the laissez faire theorists say that suppliers work hard to sell their products or services for one reason: to make a profit. Go on to introduce the concept of a market economy by quoting from Adam Smith, who said "It is not from the benevolence of the butcher, the brewer, or the baker that we expect our dinner, but from their regard to their own self-interest."[80] To make a profit and to satisfy their own self-interest, however, they must provide what the market wants. Therefore, in Adam Smith's market economy, everyone benefits, both producers and buyers. When both parties are free to choose what they sell and what they buy, the "invisible hand" of competition guides the market so that the personal initiative of, and indeed the greed of, the suppliers combine to produce an overall collective gain.[81] There is no government interference giving us a handout. As Milton Friedman so eloquently stated it, "There's no such thing as 'a free lunch.' If the government spends a dollar, that dollar has to come from producers and workers in the private economy. There is no magical 'multiplier effect' by taking from productive Peter and giving to unproductive Paul."[82]

I would also point out Milton Friedman's belief that "'Higher taxes never reduce the deficit. Government spends whatever they take in and then whatever they can get away with.'"[82] and his claim that to make America more prosperous, we should do three things: "'promote free trade, school choice for all children, and cut government spending.'"[82]

Then I would give the opposing theory with a statement to the effect that countering the laissez faire argument, there is the theory of the government acting as a visible hand (or "handout," some detractors would say), espoused by Keynes and Krugman. They argue that even in a sound, growing, ordered economy, there will be times when unanticipated internal or external forces temporarily slow down, halt, or even reverse this pattern of growth. And it is at these times that government must intervene to help right the ship.[83] Accordingly, in recessionary times the government should spend on job-producing programs and projects in order to stimulate growth; conversely, when the economy is expanding the government should step back, spend less, pay down debt, and save for the future.[84]

And here we could take another look at "freedom," as discussed previously, but with an additional twist. In addition to the freedoms applicable to our individual lives as addressed in the previous discussion of America's mission and vision, there are other very important freedoms that govern the overall economic and social well-being of us collectively. Take free markets. Even

Adam Smith, saw inherent limits based on equity. Writing in *The Wealth of Nations*, his magnum opus published in 1776, Smith declared, "No society can surely be flourishing and happy, of which the far greater part of the members are poor and miserable. It is but equity, besides, that they who feed, cloth, and lodge the whole body of people, should have such a share of the produce of their own labour as to be themselves tolerably well fed, clothed and lodged." He called for "wages that cover the cost of living according to the standards of the day."[85]

And surely no man can be considered truly free if the society and culture in which he lives does not afford him with a wage that fairly compensates him for his efforts and contribution to his community. Unfortunately, this is the situation for many living and working in the nation with the world's strongest economy. These are those performing what we labeled and all agreed are services "essential" to our well being in good times and bad, in times of low unemployment and smooth sailing as well as in times of social and economic challenges and rough seas. I'm talking about the grocers, delivery drivers, farm workers, caregivers, nursing assistants and other trades who put in all those extra hours risking their health to keep the country going during the COVID19 pandemic. If they are so essential, couldn't we do better than the median pay of $14.25 that nursing assistants and orderlies see or the $12 to $14 of the typical farmworker. Shouldn't we be able to offer a single day of paid sick leave to the majority of nursing and home health aides[86]

Dr. Martin Luther King, Jr., asserting the dignity of all work when addressing racial inequality, asked, "What does it profit a man to be able to eat at an integrated lunch counter if he doesn't earn enough money to buy a hamburger?" And President Theodore Roosevelt perhaps expressed it best when he argued for a "living wage" that was high enough "to provide for education and recreation, to care for immature members of the family, to maintain the family during periods of sickness, and to permit of reasonable saving for old age."[86]

The written lecture handout for this lesson on economic theories could be something as simple as the above few paragraphs.

A second lecture could address the role of deficits and debt in our national and global financial health. Since, at this time and for the foreseeable future, there does not appear to be any opportunity to balance our budgets and chip away at our debt, this discussion would revolve around "how much can we support." Up until very recently the thinking apparently has been that as the debt approaches or exceed 100 percent of our Gross Domestic Product, we totter on the brink of calamity. As we piled on debt in 2020, however, that 100 percent limit was being questioned:

- Can we keep this Ponzi scheme going by merely increasing GDP? Is growth, therefore, the key to our economy, or, as I tend to think, does growth for growth's sake merely accelerate the overuse and waste of our resources and the destruction of our planet?

- Since the Federal Reserve in times like the COVID-19 pandemic buys most of the increases in debt securities that the Treasury sells, there is no public claim on this debt, and both the creditor and debtor are essentially the same, the federal government, only different pockets.
- The United States borrows in its own currency minimizing the risk of a sovereign debt crisis.
- In some period of heavy borrowing, for example during the COVID-19 pandemic, interest rates are close to zero.
- At the end of World War II, the U.S. public debt was in excess of GDP with no adverse consequences.

These realities make for a challenging lecture!

A third lecture might be organized around a brief discussion of our place in the global economy, focusing on the pros and cons of trade agreements and the role of imports and exports in our domestic economy, and perhaps a discussion of the legitimate assigned fiscal responsibilities of governments.

And a fourth lecture might focus on the responsibilities of corporations. Are they solely bound, as Milton Friedman in his 1970 manifesto wrote, to their shareholders or other owners, with the portion of the profits distributed for the common good through taxation determined by the government or through philanthropy? Or are corporations directly responsible to all their stakeholders, employees, suppliers, their community and the environment as well as their owners, as the leaders of many large socially responsible corporations and much of the general public believe? *The New York Times* published on September 13, 2020 a special magazine section on this subject, "GREED IS GOOD. EXCEPT WHEN IT'S BAD"[87] including Friedman's article and the opinions of many of his detractors that would be a good reference for this lecture.

With this kind of introduction to economic theory, our participants would get just enough to understand the broad concepts; for some of them it will serve to whet their appetites to learn more, aided by the recommended reading list handed out at the conclusion of the course.

Introduction to Taxes, Health Insurance, and Retirement Benefit

Next, let's give our students a basic understanding of the how's and why's of their financial lives. For starters, let's take the mystery out of income taxes. The difference between effective and marginal tax rates shouldn't be confusing to the taxpayer, but it frequently is. I recall an employee refusing a raise I offered because it would put him in a higher tax bracket. I had a hard time explaining that only the raised portion would be taxed at the higher rate.

While we're at it, let's have a conversation with our participants about where our taxes go. Let's be sure they know how every citizen, rich or poor, benefits from the investments made possible through taxes, including transportation and utility networks, scientific and medical research, defense capabilities, national parks, education, regulatory agencies, social safety nets, and environmental protections.

Let's also be sure that they understand the rationale behind our various tax deductions—why the federal government has built into the tax code certain inducements to make us all participants in our communities: the inducement to buy a house (the mortgage deduction); to give to charitable causes we believe in (charitable deductions); to further education (the student loan deduction); and so on. Designed to incentivize social and economic growth and stability, these deductions have worked brilliantly for decades, though they may now need some updating.

What do we mean by "subsidies," "tax deductions," and "entitlements"? What are the intended purposes and effects of them on the social and economic health of our country? Are these incentives and benefits fairly distributed to and shared by the underprivileged, the middle class, the "upper 1 percent," by small businesses and corporate giants? Surely a little education along these lines would go a long way toward building a more enlightened electorate to combat the inequities that regularly creep into our tax code and need reform.

Our participants also should be introduced to pension, disability and retirement concepts and how to make the right choices in health care insurance to fit their individual circumstances. They will be better and more secure citizens, more selective voters, and more likely to involve themselves in policy issues in the future if they really understand what is at stake.

Personal Finances

An introduction to personal finances also would be invaluable and absolutely must be absorbed before striking out on one's own to invest in property or financial assets or in further education, to earn a living, or to start a family. A survey conducted by the Council for Economic Education disclosed that only 21 states (2020 figure) require a standalone or even an integrated course in personal finances. Bruce Adams, President and CEO of the Credit Union League of Connecticut, bemoaned the fact that his state does not. In his article about making "financial literacy a graduation requirement," he noted that, while some of his credit union members understand their financial realities, others are stressed, anxious and uncertain about how to survive. He said that successfully confronting life's increasingly difficult financial decisions would be much easier for those who had learned to save, pay for college education, invest and spend knowledgeably, and budget for emergencies as well as daily expenses.

Some of this knowledge is being imparted by Connecticut credit unions through financial reality fairs offered to high school students, 30,000 of whom have been reached.[88]

For a high school or college course workable model, I would suggest that the curriculum designers turn to Champlain College in Vermont. The college has developed the Center for Financial Literacy with a unique curriculum for students, teachers and all adults across Vermont. The Center's stated goal is to increase "knowledge of money matters [so that] college students graduate with the skills to make sound decisions about spending, credit and investments, and help adults navigate difficult financial situations like buying a home and saving for retirement."[89]

John Pelletier, Director of Champlain's Center, explains that "The Great Recession demonstrated that our citizens struggle when making complex financial decisions that are critical to their well-being. Some of our economic problems were created by bad actors, focused on personal gain, but so many others were created by good people making poorly-informed personal financial decisions."[90]

Pelletier notes that "we would not allow a young person to get in the driver's seat of a car without requiring driver's education, and yet we allow our citizens to enter the complex financial world without any related education. An uneducated individual armed with a credit card, a student loan, and access to a mortgage can be nearly as dangerous to themselves and their community as a person with no training who is given a car to drive."[90]

Champlain College's plan includes courses on budgeting and goal-setting, understanding credit, sound investing, understanding employee benefits, repaying student loans, and buying the first car. And, in addition to spreading their programs throughout Vermont, the Center is also advocating for similar educational opportunities at other local and state levels, as well as the national level. Other states, colleges, and institutions are also exploring ways to improve financial literacy. Bank of America in partnership with Khan Academy has developed a free on-line education course, Better Money Habits, addressing payroll deductions, taxes, saving, etc.[91] However, as yet, a huge gap in financial literacy still remains, particularly among the disadvantaged.

Perhaps the most basic element of personal finances needed is in decision-making. How much income do I need to accomplish my goals? The typical answer would be rather surprising to most. For example, a *USA Today* report in 2014 determined that it required an income of over $130,000 for a family of four to afford a middle class lifestyle that includes home ownership, two cars, adequate health insurance, college education for two children, an annual family vacation, and adequate retirement planning.[92] Obviously by 2020 this figure has increased, especially since the cost of some of these basics has exceeded inflation. The recession of 2009 was brought about in great part by the bursting of the housing bubble, revealing the woeful ignorance of so many new home buyers about the obligations and consequences of the mortgage documents they signed.

Friedman and Mandelbaum wrote about it in *That Used to be Us.* "High-risk home buyers ... were sometimes actually encouraged to lie about their incomes—or lack of them. The broker told the family assuming the mortgage that …if they couldn't meet the monthly payments when they started kicking in, no problem. Just walk away from the property— 'you'll be gone—or sell it for a profit because, as we all knew' at the time, housing prices would keep going up forever. They would never go down."[93] Really? The lessons to be taught and learned in a course on financial literacy could easily be included in our education curriculum. Had such been done in our schools, how many foreclosures, how much destruction of the housing market, how much emotional pain and suffering, could have been avoided?

Making a Living

Now, given that creativity and innovation are the drivers of our future, how about teaching our young participants some basic lessons in how to make money? Steve Mariotti knows something about this. He founded the Network for Teaching Entrepreneurship, a nonprofit organization "that helps young people from low-income communities unlock their potential for entrepreneurial creativity by teaching them to start their own businesses."[94] Bill Gross also has explored this kind of educational opportunity for young people. Gross is the founder of IdeaLab, "an innovation laboratory that supports 'groundbreaking companies whose products and services change the way people think, live and work.'"[95] Gross claims that "the biggest barrier to creativity…is 'lack of self-confidence.'"[96] This course will surely help our students boost their confidence.

Other Life Preparation Courses

Our program could also educate our youngsters on subjects as diverse as health and diet issues and the role of labor unions in our economy and society. Some basic tutoring in civilized behavior—what used to be called "manners" and getting along with your neighbors—would be advisable too.

The sad fact is that we are becoming a nation of boors. Imagine the enormous toll taken on human capital and the detriment to society occasioned by the unruly behavior and lax discipline in our schools. This must be an underlying cause of the advocacy for charter schools and the promotion of school vouchers. Unfortunately, this can only contribute in the long run to the further deterioration of the public school system by diverting public funding to new, often church-based, private schools. We like to think that civilized behavior is the sole responsibility of parents.

Some of them do a commendable job, but many of them do not. Some school teachers succeed here, but many do not, one of the main reasons being that they are not supported by the administrators who, in turn are not supported by school boards who succumb to the pressure of influential parent groups. The only facet of society that seems to stress courtesy and civilized behavior is the military. They set an excellent example for their recruits and enforce it, and this can be copied in other learning experiences.

Caring and Courtesy

Military courtesy is one of the defining features of the professional force. These courtesies form a strict and sometimes elaborate code of conduct, derived from courtesies once practiced in everyday life. They are intended to reinforce discipline and to conform with the chain of command, one more way in which soldiers are instructed to treat their superiors and vice versa. Military courtesies include proper forms of address and when and where to salute, as well as proper wear of military uniform and head gear, and the rules of behavior relating to particular ceremonies. The rules are made clear through strict and consistent enforcement.

I'm not suggesting that our youth be required to give a hand salute to their parents, teachers and other elders and community members, but if training in courtesy comportment and dress fits in with the military experience, it should fit in as one of our lessons.

Look around. In public events, when the national anthem is played, most of us stand. Some of the exceptions are those who kneel, exercising their Constitutional rights in protesting not the flag but some social injustice. On the other hand, you will note that many, standing or kneeling, do not place their right hand or hat over their heart as required. Is this a big deal? Yes!

Not everyone will agree on what constitutes proper behavior, and, to be sure, what constituted proper courtesy, comportment, and dress 50 or 100 years ago might not always be suitable in today's social environment. Regardless, while not everyone will make the current preferred practices, whatever they are, a permanent part of their social behavior, the training can't hurt and for some it will become ingrained practice.

We all have some "pet peeves" regarding the uncaring attitude of some of our citizenry, for example the shopping cart left in the middle of a grocery store parking space, beer cans and fast food trash discarded along our country roads, or the purposely unmuffled noise of a hot rod cruising our streets. This disrespect for others has magnified significantly over the past decades. With our curriculum in place, we will have an opportunity to take a look at the past and perhaps to return to yesteryear, if, on review, we find that today's traditional ways of interacting don't quite measure up.

We even see uncaring attitude affecting our personal social life interactions. Plan a party, cookout, or wedding for more than just your close friends and see how many leave you guessing about their attendance, unheard of in the past. Then again how about those who accept a party invitation or date and then cancel at the last minute or simply never show up because they have a conflict that they didn't consider or because they're too busy with more important things. David Brooks in an article in *The New York Times* described this disregard for commitments, "bailing" as it is now labeled, as indicative of an overall collapse of social relations. It even extends to a degree to business relationships typically expressed by those in a superior position bailing on a lower status colleague.[97]

And perhaps the most egregious example of a lack of caring for others came about recently when municipalities, states and colleges and universities came out of lockdown as cases slowed in the first wave of the COVID-19 pandemic.

As I described in Chapter Five, vast numbers resumed socializing in large groups paying little or no attention to social distancing and face mask requirements. This was in blatant disregard, not only for their own safety, but the safety of others, particularly the older generations including their grandparents, and the frontline healthcare workers who would be exposed to those whose irresponsible behavior caused them to fall victim to the virus. There's a role to be played here by our lessons. Perhaps we can help reverse this trend.

The Art of Compromise
As indicated in the beginning of this chapter, this lesson is found in Chapter Nine.

Anticipating the Future
Lastly, we have been talking about lessons that relate to issues with which we currently grapple, every day for most of us. But, as our younger students grow, there is a good chance that they will eventually be faced with a concern or concerns that do not presently rise to the level of a major issue. How many of us adults, especially

seniors, would have ever considered in our earlier years that someday some of the most serious challenges to us, to the future of mankind in fact, would be climate change or racial injustice and inequality. Actually, we need only open our eyes a little wider when we look around us to come up with some very serious current potential issues or practices which we tend to overlook, but which, as Nicholas Kristof pointed out in a *New York Times* article, "our great-grandchildren will find bewilderingly immoral about our own times—and about us." Mr. Kristof identified as one issue the "cruelty to animals" citing factory farming practices, specifically the brutal processes that we use to slaughter poultry, cattle and other domesticated animals, let alone the cruel crowded conditions in which we raise many of them, poultry and calves for example. A generation or two from now, when many if not most of us conclude that the human race is merely the highest in a progressive order of animal life, and not distinctly different from a sensory stand-point from others high in the order, elephants and whales for example, will they be horrified by the way previous generations treated others of the animal order.[98]

Another, and much more egregious example would be the indifference demonstrated by those of us in the developed countries to the unimaginable suffering of those in impoverished countries. We seem to have no concept of the malnutrition, lack of shelter and inadequate healthcare of the millions, especially children living a barely survivable existence. Yes, we contribute to charities that feed and otherwise care for the poor, but when we put our checkbook away, most of us merely resume our daily habits. Hopefully it will be a way of life for future generations to automatically devote part of their life to service, likely in a national service program as we have discussed. Will they look back at us and say, "Why didn't we do more to alleviate suffering?"[98]

And thirdly, of course, as future generation still suffer from the havoc we have raised with our planet, battling damaging climate occurrences that threaten their food supply and health, will they ask why, although we had all the tools to do it, did we not do more to reduce or control the threat?[98]

Before leaving all of these recommendations about what should be considered when the experts create the course outlines and lesson plans for our curriculum, let's make sure that, when the lessons end, the messages continue to resonate. Summer reading lists still exist in our better school systems, and lengthy course-related reading assignments are common at our colleges and universities. So it should be with our courses each of which would end with a recommended reading list. Follow-through would be voluntary, but I would guess that a good percentage of our students would take the challenge, if not right away, then at some later stage of life. These books could be the beginning of a new 21st century common core of "classic" literature, serving much the same purpose today as reading the Greek and Roman scholars and philosophers did for our forebears.

Chapter Seven
Where and When Do we Learn These Lessons?

The roots of education are bitter, but the fruits are sweet.

Aristotle

Let's pause for a minute to summarize what we're trying to accomplish with our somewhat different approach to education. In simplest terms, the lessons learned in our PreK through 12 curriculum and reinforced in our national service basic training are intended to transform us into better and engaged citizens and also to ease the path to productive and rewarding employment or to any post secondary learning or training to that end. Any post secondary education prior to employment should focus only on courses directly applicable to that employment if unmanageable college tuition debt is to be avoided.

Common Core for a Citizen Corps

Now let's look at the chronology of the specific steps that we take to incorporate all of these lessons into the education process as we develop our Common Core for a Citizen Corps so that, with everyone equally educated in our lessons, we are able to break the barrier between the elites and the working class—everyone is equal—regardless of the rest of their education—when we do look at the rest of the education there is no superiority between being an expert in HVAC learned at a trade school or through an apprenticeship, being a mid level assistant at a financial or tech firm using the background of our citizenship common core, or being a scholar of Russian history learned at a university. The knowledge learned in our lessons puts everyone on an even footing conversing at a cocktail party or a town meeting, HVAC or Russian history rarely a subject of discussion at same. You don't need a college education to be an exemplary citizen, educated, enlightened, and just as "elite" as anyone else. If you have a firm grasp of the lessons in this book, you can hold your own in any social gathering. Many of the lessons can capture the interest of the "student" and lead to a life long commitment related to the particular course, just as though in a much more limited student audience a course in one of the liberal arts might start the student on the way to a lifelong crusade.

Life Skills—Four Cs

While many holders of bachelor's degrees may not have put to use any specific course knowledge gained at college, many of us, myself included, have supported a liberal arts education for those who are prepared, serious and enthusiastic when choosing this path as a means to attain critical general purpose life skills and appreciation of different cultures and the artistic as well as natural wonders of the world. These skills have been identified by many authors and scholars as the "four Cs'—critical thinking, communication, collaboration and creativity."[99] And, as we encounter and grapple with the innovation and rapid changes of the technical revolution, artificial intelligence, and media and algorithms that can "manipulate your emotions with uncanny precision,"[100] these skills will continue to be more critical in helping us to achieve a meaningful and productive life. However, the four-year college experience is hardly the only way to achieve these skills. In fact, many of these skills must be at least partially developed in order to even gain entrance to, and profit from, the offerings of, a four-year college.

For example, communication skills should start in early childhood and pre-K when the parents and teachers tell you to "speak up" or "explain yourself" when they read or tell you a story, when you express your preference for what you would like to read, and when you are told to take your turn in a home or classroom setting. Then, as detailed for example in the Common Core for State Standards for those states that incorporate it, in primary through middle school, we develop our reading and comprehension habits, our writing skills, and hopefully we attain the basics in public speaking giving oral reports in front of our classmates. This all continues in high school, with the better students participating in debates, soliciting donations in local fund raisers, and writing book reports and essays.

The requirement for critical thinking, collaboration and creativity as well as communication skills as curricula foundations are all extensively detailed in the Common

Core Standards. Below are my step by step recommendations covering our curriculum's new or increased focus. Throughout the later steps, of course, there must be a concerted continuous effort by the educators—be they parents, school teachers, professors, or any other mentors—to make sure that their students differentiate between evidence based science and faith based or political party based beliefs. Without this, and looking at the extremes, we and our government will continue to stumble along with no consensus on the critical issues. For example, because of its primary focus on the short term economy, one of our two major parties remains in denial about the consequences of man made contribution to climate change, or, for that matter, in denial about something as basic as evolution because of the fear of losing the support of its evangelical base.[101]

Early Childhood—Parents—Pre-K — and Other Mentors

Here is where the keys to becoming enlightened citizens and voters start—a family environment that makes time for reading to the children, that makes time for having meals together and discussing the children's activities, desires, needs and relationships with friends and neighbors. During these days, appreciation for the benefits of home, community and nation can be instilled. Knowledge about how people in other lands live can be taught and comparisons made with our way of life.

In our fragmented society, many if not most families in the upper echelons do well here. However, in the disadvantaged communities we fall down. Low wages in unskilled jobs mandate two earners to keep afloat. With husband and wife working long hours, maintaining this type of family environment is almost impossible. Children after school may have to pretty much fend for themselves, often making their own meals, leaving just enough time for homework. Alternatively, unsupervised, that same time may be spent hanging out with gangs and in other antisocial behavior.

Living Income for Families with Children

One of these answers here, of course, is to regulate our economy and fiscal policy so that more of these unskilled jobs pay a living wage enabling one of the parents to be at home nurturing their children, raising the minimum wage being one approach. Another answer being constantly espoused by progressives is to drastically increase the child care credit to adequately cover all expenses related either to the child care provided by a paid caretaker or to adequately compensate the stay-at-home partner for the care that he or she provides, i.e. laundry, cooking, cleaning, training, reading, activities, etc. Any stay-at-home mother or father as the case may be will tell you that this is hard work, just as exhausting, if not more so, as most lower or middle wage jobs. And here is another justification that we all tend to forget— the contribution to society by bearing and raising the children required to supply needed, young, healthy workers to replace our aging population and sustain our economy without relying solely on a growing and needed influx of immigrants. The birth-rate in the United States is now down to 1.73. As Kim Brooks states in her opinion piece "Forget Pancakes. Pay Women": "If raising these future citizens isn't socially necessary labor, I'm not sure what is."[102]

These answers to the question of how do we encourage a stay-at-home parent to properly raise and guide children in their earliest most impressionable years would not have the disadvantage of killing work incentive that an unconditional guaranteed minimum income as proposed by political commentator and 2020 Democratic presidential hopeful Andrew Yang and some other progressives favor.

Why is it that, up until the 1960s, with the exception of the early 1940s when the men went off to war and many of the women worked on the home front in factories or performed other services in support of the war effort, that the traditional family had only one working parent, typically the male, with the other parent staying home raising the children? Yes, I know, we can come up with a myriad of explanations for this, but I would contend that, without our obsessive concern with growing the GDP, there has only been so much production and service labor required, and in the past it was accomplished by one worker, yet now it is done by two. And this in spite of the fact that robots and other automation and technology has significantly reduced the work load, and will continue to do so. We now worry about how to pay those idled by automation. I say let's increase the pay scale so that one family member can, if they wish, indeed support the family as in the past. This may, and in fact should, halt or at least slow our ever-increasing focus on growing the GDP that relies on growing the thirst for more and more new clothes, fancy vacations, expensive gas guzzling cars, and the latest electronic devices for all of our children including toddlers. Put an end to our excessive consumerism. Put an end to our throw-away society. And, yes, if we stop growing our economy for the sake of growth, we will have to, and will be able to, control our spending and even reduce the debt burden.

Perhaps we should also put to bed the idea that owning one's home, specifically a "big house," is critical to the American dream—maybe for some but not for all. In other developed parts of the world, western Europe for example, many of the middle class live happily in rental apartments and homes, quite modest from our standpoint, and get along quite nicely relying on the landlord for all but relatively minor maintenance. When we homeowners spend our weekends mowing the lawn, many middle class western European renters spend theirs sailing or fishing at a cabin on the lake, in the woods or on the mountains.

Step back and smell the roses. There can be better ways to "keep up with the Jones's."

Now, let me make myself perfectly clear. I am not arguing for the return of the day when all the husbands and fathers went off to work and the wives and mother stayed home cleaning house and looking after the children. I would look forward to the day when the roles are relatively equal. For the spouse staying at home in today's environment, there are a myriad of part-time volunteer opportunities that badly require filling. Regardless, if both parents wish to work and they can make satisfactory arrangements for the children, fine, but economic considerations should not force them to.

Those couples who admirably both wish to pursue satisfying and or socially productive careers away from home who also choose to have children must realize that it will be difficult, and extra effort will be required to make up for the negative effects on the children of their limited parenting. Very selective day care that will truly provide a learning environment, not just baby sitting, and/or shortened working hours for one of the parents are two possibilities.

Now in many disadvantaged communities, one of the parents, typically the father, is taken out of the equation due to incarceration. This is particularly prevalent in communities dominated by persons of color, and due in great part to our broken judicial system in which persons of color are many times more likely to be incarcerated than whites for similar infractions, many if not most related to drug use or trafficking. Judicial reforms to correct this are being considered and implemented, especially in the wake of the Black Lives Matter movement, but we have a long way to go.

With the time available from parents and/or day care some of the very basics of our lessons in living courses could begin in early childhood and pre-K. In the typical pre-K setting, children are taught, with hands-on materials, songs and games, to count, to identify colors, numerals, sizes and shapes, recognize letters and sounds, understand and appreciate stories, to create a picture by painting and drawing, and much more. They begin to learn basic social skills working together, sharing classroom materials, taking care of their basic cleaning and clothing needs, and much more that could readily include the basics of some of our lessons, e.g. Caring and Courtesy or the recommendations for avoiding waste spelled out in the Environmental Protection lesson.[103]

W. Steven Barnett of the National Institute for Early Education Research in his paper "Preschool Education and its Lasting Effects: Research and Policy Implications" arrived at the following conclusions, touting the benefits of preschool programs but at the same time disparaging some of the current public policies:

- "Many different preschool programs have been shown to produce positive effects on children's learning and development...."
- "Well-designed preschool education programs produce long-term improvements in school success, including higher achievement test scores, lower rates of grade repetition and special education, and higher educational attainment. Some preschool programs are also associated with

reduced delinquency and crime in childhood and adulthood."

- "The strong evidence suggests that economically disadvantaged children reap long-term benefits from preschool. However, children from all other socioeconomic backgrounds have been found to benefit as well."
- "Current public policies for child care, Head Start, and state pre-K, do not ensure that most American children will attend highly effective preschool programs. Some attend no program at all, and others attend educationally weak programs. Children from middle-income families have least access, but many children in poverty also lack preschool experiences."
- "Increasing child care subsidies under current federal and state policies is particularly unlikely to produce any meaningful improvements in children's learning and development. Given the poor quality of much child care, it might instead produce mild negative consequences."
- "Increasing public investment in effective preschool education programs for all children can produce substantial educational, social and economic benefits...."
- "Publicly funded pre-K for all might produce a paradoxical but worthwhile effect in terms of educational gains. Disadvantaged children benefit (in comparison to their gains with targeted programs), but so do more advantaged children."[104]

Even in pre-K, as in all other phases of education, the digital age provides learning apps that can be accessed in school or at home, some with and some without teacher or parent guidance. In today's environment what better way to encourage youngsters to learn. For example, *Bedtime Math* involves word problems of interest to ages 3 and up that develop basic math skills, this particular app having received peer review and been shown to boost math scores later on. Another app, *The Human Body,* aimed at ages 5 and up, moves around the body demonstrating the functions of different organs, and another one, of particular fun for pre-K, *A Kid's Diary,* acts like social media except with the activities restricted to those of the child and the family. All of these are a great way for a parent to enhance the learning process—but a parent or other suitable teacher must be there![105]

K through 8 and High School

What would we like to accomplish before we can introduce our new core curriculum into our K through high school primary and secondary education curriculum?

Where across the globe do we find the most successful education programs, the real role models. Most would look to Scandinavia, in particular Finland with its "bildung" model as described in Chapter Five. And the experts all seem to attribute much of their success to the quality of the teachers who are at the top of the pay scale and held in high esteem. Only the most talented embark on this career. Here in America, on the other hand, our public school teachers, while they may have a have a degree in education, in many cases are not those who have graduated from college with honors in English, math, history or any of the other subjects that they end up teaching. As a society, we must support compensation, both in paycheck and esteem, that encourages our most talented to enter the teaching profession.

Present conditions surely discourage many who would like to enter the profession. In a *New York Times* opinion piece by Alexandra Robbins, a San Antonio teacher making $30,000 who strives to make ends meet by working as a carpet cleaner from 4 to 7 p.m. after his teaching day closes, said, "I'm always thinking, 'How am I going to feed my family?'" Over the 2010-20 decade, the national average teacher salary has dropped 4.5 percent adjusted for inflation.[106] To be sure, the compensation is better in some parts of the country, the Northeast for example, than in others, the Southeast for example.

The situation under the Trump administration and Education Secretary Betsy DeVos deteriorated to the point where public education has been belittled, funding for teacher training and support and to reduce class size has been cut, and harassment and even assault of teachers is not adequately addressed. Mr. Trump and Ms. DeVos repeatedly attempted to divert funding from public schools to private programs instead of using the funds to improve the public system. Even high school students see the teachers' struggle and don't want that life. A 2010 Phi Delta Kappa poll found that "about half the country's public school teachers—and 61 percent of high school teachers—had seriously considered quitting the profession in the past few years." The majority of teachers in this poll said that their schools were underfunded, they were unfairly paid, and they would vote to strike for better funding. In this, the wealthiest nation on earth, teachers frequently have to use their own money to buy needed classroom supplies. Overcoming these funding conditions shouldn't take a strike.[106]

Teachers are arguably the most valuable hard working members of our work force, yet they are among the most underappreciated and overworked. When asked what they want the next administration to address, restoring respect for the profession was among the most frequent answers. Unfortunately, many of us are not aware of how bleak the situation is. A poll of Democratic voters asked them which candidate in the 2020 Democratic primary would best handle health care, climate change, foreign policy and immigration—not a word about education.[106]

Raising teachers' qualifications, paychecks and esteem will create the foundation on which all levels of education rest, and this must be the foundation for our new core curriculum with its lessons in living. The courses will all be additions to, or replacements for, courses in the traditional K through high-school grades. If there is no room in current curricula to fit them in, then they should replace any of the existing courses with the exception of the mathematics courses and all courses in reading, writing and speaking which must not be eliminated. Some of the courses will have lessons taught at all levels, elementary, middle and high school, others at two levels and others perhaps at only one. I envision them as required, not elective. On graduation from high school, in addition to a high school diploma, the graduate will receive a Certificate of Satisfactory Completion of Lessons in Living. On the other hand, if the states or school districts choose to consider these courses as electives, those graduates not having satisfactorily completed all of them will not receive the applicable Certificate, but they will receive a transcript indicating specifically which lessons in living they have satisfactorily completed. The reasons for these Certificates and transcripts will become apparent in Chapter Eleven where we discuss the associate's and bachelor's degrees in Citizenship.

Reinforced with Condensed Version in the Basic Training Phase of our Universal National Service Program

Another suitable time to absorb these lessons would be if and when it could be included as a vital component of the basic training period of both the military and civilian service options of a mandatory national service program, about which I wrote in *Step Forward America!* However, at this time it appears that any national service program, as recommended by the National Commission on Military, National and Public Service, and any subsequent bill enacted by Congress, will be voluntary.

And it will not include a one-size-fits-all basic training session or any other feature requiring all participants to live and work together in a group that would be conducive to supporting this education element.

Should we eventually have a mandatory national service program with our lessons in living incorporated in the basic training, that would obviate the need for the school systems to include courses in most of the related subjects. Regardless, civics and media literacy courses cannot wait until after graduation from high school and should be included in their curriculum. Granted, there probably would be among our universal service participants a modest number who are already thoroughly versed in most if not all of these basics through courses in some high schools and other learning experiences. They might bypass the educational phase and more quickly go on to their national military, national civilian, or international humanitarian service assignment.

In sum, our lessons learned in primary and secondary education and reinforced in the basic training phase of our universal national service program will help immeasurably in getting all of our youth off to a better start in adult life, whether they go on to college, a trade school, or directly into the workplace. These courses will both further their marketability and create a foundation for good citizenship. We will have helped immeasurably to overcome the complaint of business that too many of our young people are ill-prepared not only to handle the technical challenges of the available jobs but also to understand the social and economic environment in which business opportunities exist. As no less a sage than Adam Smith, the 18th century proponent of *laissez faire* market mechanisms, observed, there is a place for government intervention in providing basic elementary education for all, on the premise that an educated populace would make better decisions and thus assist the "invisible hand" on behalf of economic growth and public well-being.

Community College-Occupational School: Stepping Stone to a Citizenship Degree

In "The Case For Community College" (*Time* magazine June 12, 2017), author Josh Sanburn makes a compelling argument for a two-year associate's degree at these institutions, not only as a stepping stone to a bachelor's degree at a four-year institution but as an occupational education and training experience leading to a meaningful and productive job and career. He pointed out that the then median salary for those with a high school diploma was $36,000, and for those with a community college degree $42,600, and he referred to President Obama's emphasis on the benefits of community colleges and his call for making them tuition free. After the Great Recession, community colleges were "seen as the primary vehicle for work-force training in this country" according to Carrie Kisker, Director for the Center for the Study of Community Colleges.[107]

Referring to the occupational schools leading to a meaningful productive job and career, Mr. Sanburn described the Lake Area Technical Institute (LATI) in Watertown, South Dakota, and their hangar-size classrooms "filled with wind turbines, solar panels, ethanol distillers and miniature hydroelectric dams." To a student he interviewed, "trigonometry began making sense when you used it to fit together piping systems. Basic computer code seemed worth learning when you could program an assembly-line robot." That student went on to a maintenance technician job at 3M starting at $60,000. LATI is a model for community colleges as an avenue for moving students up the social and economic ladder. In 2016, a full 99 percent of its graduates went right into the workforce or on to a four year college. It has an 83 percent retention rate, and few of its students default on their loans. Its success can be attributed in part to their partnership with local businesses around whose needs they shape their curriculum, and from whom they rely on donations of equipment. Demand and enrollments are growing. Unfortunately, however, the typical community college does not enjoy similar success. Enrollments and budgets are sinking. As of 2017, graduation rates on average are less than 40 percent, and, while 80 percent of community college students want a bachelor's degree, only 14 percent achieve it after six years.[107] Some states, of course, do a better job than others. In California and New York, for example, programs are available offering free tuition based on financial need.

Hopefully, the current administration will adopt tuition assistance for all based on need, amounting to free tuition or a very modest fee for the neediest, at publicly funded community college. This is an important option in this rounded plan for a childhood to maturity education that provides our necessary lessons in living curriculum with its comprehensive back-ground in civics, and for a path toward productive employment that is required of an enlightened electorate.

Another option that has received little or no attention, might be a standalone-one semester program at community colleges devoted solely to our lessons in living, preferably before or after a national service year—another excellent path to good citizenship, or if desired, a degree in citizenship.

At times of low unemployment, what are the jobs most in demand? These are typically those that require some degree of technical skills not possessed by the typical college grad looking to put to use their costly bachelor's degrees and start paying off their tuition debt. Those on the other hand who do have these skills are those who have availed themselves of government registered apprenticeships offering on the job training combined with educational courses. Some of our lessons could be added to the education courses typically included in apprenticeship training. Those enrolled in these apprenticeships receive some income while developing skills in various mechanical, electrical and plumbing trades. These are common in construction but also available in other industries. On completion of the apprenticeship programs, the majority obtain jobs with starting salaries exceeding those of most four year college graduates.

Of course, in the long run, those who make good use of their college degree have financial opportunities not available to those with only an apprenticeship. But as we know all too well, many are not suited for four years of liberal arts or scientific study and many of those who do manage to obtain a degree are not successful in putting it to good use.[108] A community college experience can lead to a degree in citizenship that they will put to good use.

Four-Year College

I have saved for last the discussion of four years of undergraduate study. I am a firm believer in the benefits of some courses in the liberal arts or sciences for many of us. College courses, in addition to providing specific knowledge about particular subjects, teach us to think and delve deeper into the subject, and develop an inquiring mind and learning habit. I contend, however, that the aforementioned learning phases that we have addressed, if fully implemented, should have already accomplished this. Critical thinking skills can, or in fact should, be taught before college, and if they are not, then successful accomplishments of college professors based on their raw student material become questionable. Each and every one of our lessons, if taught in the manner I recommend, addressing the arguments from both or all sides of the issues—what better way to develop critical thinking skills?

Therefore, should one have a thirst for learning specific subjects beyond what they have been taught in the aforementioned steps, they can quench this thirst at any time without devoting four years to pursuit of a degree. Ideally, everyone should have a basic familiarity with philosophy and art history, would have an appreciation of the fine performing and visual arts that contribute to the quality of life, and would have an understanding of the basics of physical laws that govern the universe and our place in it. But online courses, libraries, museums, local adult education courses, etc., provide ample opportunities for these throughout life for those who are lacking in them and wish to pursue them.

To be sure, four years of college can be a marvelous life-changing experience with opportunities to pursue existing passions or explore new ones, career-related or not, but this is not for all, and we don't need to spend untold sums to fully fund two- or four-year tuition for all as proposed by Bernie Sanders, Elizabeth Warren and the other extreme progressives in the Democratic Party. Even if we did as a nation decide that a college education was indeed critical for most of us in order to advance our careers, four or even two years of additional time after high school sheltered from the challenges of the real world would represent simply a free ride for many—a license to spend those years satisfying urges other than their thirst for knowledge—the ultimate enabling of our youth!

Many of us do not need a liberal arts or science degree to get ahead in life, and the sooner we wake up to this fact, the better. Corporate America must get on board, must stop overvaluing or even demanding a degree, sometimes only from the highest institutes of learning, the Ivies and Stanfords of the academic world, to obtain employment for which the specific undergraduate course of study may have absolutely no relevance.

The first step in waking up would be to change hiring practices to focus on job skills rather than degrees attained. This would go a long way toward expanding opportunities for those in low paying jobs, including minorities where the issue is more imminent. Research showed that 67 percent of openings for new production supervisors in 2015 included college degree requirements, whereas only 16 percent of existing production supervisors had bachelor's degrees. Have management and human resources really determined that lack of a degree has hampered the existing supervisors in their performance?[109]

A National Bureau of Economic Research study addressed the 71 million U.S. workers who have high school diplomas but no four-year degree, and whose job experience suggests that they are "skilled through alternative routes" thereby labeled by the acronym STARS. Sixteen million of them "have the skills for high-wage work, defined as earning more than twice the national median. Yet 11 million of them are currently employed in low-wage or middle-wage work."[109]

The research suggests that companies should "look for talent where STARS work and learn" and that they "hire for skills and work experience, not degrees."[109] Indeed, how many of you really put to good use your liberal arts or even your undergraduate science degrees in your first employment, or, for that matter, in your entire career? Don't count the doors that it may have opened for you to get that first job!

It's not only corporate America that has to wake up to the type of education required to "get the job done." Michael J. Sandel, a professor of government at Harvard, in a *New York Times* piece decried the fact that "very few members of the working class ever make it to elective office." While about half of our labor force is employed in manual labor, the service industry and clerical jobs, "fewer than 2 percent of members of Congress worked in such jobs before their election." He claims that "history suggests little correlation between the capacity for political judgement and the ability to win admission to elite universities." If we focus on the "capacity for political judgement," surely our lessons in living would be as conducive as most college courses in the humanities and science.[110]

I have read the argument in response to those who make a case for undergraduates studying history, and it's a good one. Understanding how our predecessors dealt with their challenges helps us deal with our own challenges, now and in the future But the cases to which we most often refer relate to today's military leaders learning from the experiences of the great military leaders of the distant past. I would leave it that, for most of us, only the history of the great events of the United States, the major wars and the social movements, as part of our civics lesson in living, would be a mandated part of our primary and secondary education.

Many, if not most, of us pursuing careers outside of the teaching, medical, legal and STEM professions, can be adequately educated to partake in the America dream without a college bachelor's degree in the arts or sciences.

Online Education

Conservatives often tell us that government is the last organization to take on the revision of our educational system, chiefly because the bureaucratic obstacles will surely stifle any new ideas. Really! Can one honestly say that a private education system that charges $100,000 to $200,000 or more to obtain a four-year college degree is doing a fine job or is a model of efficiency? Are we comfortable that today's average graduate enters the job market owing $25,000 in tuition loans with no realistic way of paying it back in a reasonable time period? Mind you that, at least under laws in effect up to 2020, the debt can't be cancelled by normal bankruptcy proceedings but only by special filings with added conditions.

Perhaps the one hope of restoring access to an affordable college education now lies in MOOCs, short for Massive Open Online Courses. Of course, these opened the door for the necessary switch to online courses as an integral part of primary, secondary and college education during the COVID-19 pandemic. Available through the Internet, MOOCs are the modern day version of correspondence courses and distance learning, two platforms that have been providing educational supplements for more than a century. The first MOOC-like multimedia courses offered in the U.S. came along in 2008, when Stanford University experimented with "An Introduction to Artificial Intelligence." Since then, MOOCs have become the fresh face of higher education, offering thousands of interactive online beginner-to-advanced courses in everything from computer programming to art history and engineering. Any student, anywhere around the globe, if they have an Internet connection (a big if) can take these courses at a time and place of his or her choosing, many of them for free. Produced by elite colleges and universities in the U.S. and abroad, they offer several weeks of classes including interactive video lectures and exercises delivered by experts in their fields. They are attracting hundreds of thousands of motivated students who see them as a path to gaining sophisticated skills without the cost of a degree.

There are now several MOOC consortiums, including edX, Udacity and Coursera, offering a constantly changing menu of teaching tools. Coursera is perhaps the largest. Its co-founder and chairman Andrew Ng, a professor of computer sciences at Stanford University, hoped to radically change higher education by lecturing to students all over the world, assigning and grading their homework, and awarding certificates for satisfactory completion of his courses to enhance their opportunities for a better job or admission to a better school. The current generation of students, already familiar with the internet, social media, smart phones and other high tech aids, are quite comfortable receiving education online, if they choose to, although somewhat less comfortable if forced to as during the COVID-19 pandemic.[111] In the beginning, Coursera students who completed the work could get a "certificate" to hang on the wall by paying a few dollars, but those early certificates were just window dressing. Now, however, with many of the kinks worked out, the bogus players have been run out of town, the quality of the best online learning has been adequately tested in the real world of work, and MOOCs may also confer "degrees" or at least college credits for successful completion.

Coursera, within its more than 4000 courses, offers many that do actually lead to a degree, including courses, taught by professors from the top colleges including the Ivies, for example "Financial Markets," "Introduction to Climate Change and Health," and "The Science of Well-Being" from Yale University, "Behavioral Finance" from Duke University, "Bonds and Stocks" from the University of Michigan, and "English for Career Development," "English for Journalism" and "Modern and Contemporary Poetry" from the University of Pennsylvania. One can obtain recognized professional certificates including their MasterTrack certificates for master's programs, and even recognized degrees that they offer. Many of their online courses are available free, and information on signing up is available on the *classcentral.com* website.[112]

Of course, when the COVID-19 pandemic arrived, most of our college students found themselves taking online courses, some for the first time, for reasons of social isolation. Naturally there was significant resistance. First of all, many of the students had a negative feeling about online courses, and, frequently, this was exacerbated when many newly offered courses were hastily conceived and developed. According to one study, 75 percent of students taking these courses didn't think they were "receiving a quality learning experience."[113] But, obviously, the pandemic provided an opportunity to not only expose the shortcomings but also to demonstrate the benefits. Faculty and administrators will ask what can we take out of this, how can we use this technology to replace some of what we're doing and how can we use it to complement what we're doing. Big lecture hall introductory classes can be very well done online, as evidenced by the very popular offerings of The Great Courses, which provides 12,000 courses in all academic disciplines on CD, DVD or in streaming form. On the other hand, duplicating online the intimacy of small group discussions led by professors passionate about their subject is difficult, and duplicating participation in the performing arts or in lab work required in science courses virtually impossible.[113]

If the pandemic has lasting effects on the perception of the value of a four-year degree, then one of the most obvious will be on the sustainability of the obscenely high tuitions charged by both public and private institutions, $100,000 for four years at the former, $200,000 or even $300,000 for the most prestigious of the latter. Hans Taparia in his "The Future of College Is Online" makes a case for "parallel" online degrees enabling universities to "expand their reach by thousands, creating the economies of scale to drop their costs by tens of thousands." This is already being done by some very prestigious schools, Georgia Tech, for example, which offers an online computer science master's degree for $7,000 or the University of Illinois, which offers an online MBA for $22,000, both a fraction of the cost of typical similar in-person graduate programs.[114]

But the pandemic switch to online courses affected not only higher education but elementary, middle and high school as well. And here many of the same concerns were undoubtedly felt. However, there is one very positive result of the switch that exposed a serious shortcoming with conventional teaching at this level, i.e. lack of discipline in the classroom. Here in person education frequently suffers. An eighth grader, in an article "Learning Online Beats School,"[115] wrote about the disruptive behavior, talking out of turn, destroying class property, disrespect for teachers, and pushing and fighting, that was common in her classroom and in so many classrooms across the nation in inner city schools and other schools in disadvantaged communities. She noted that one of her teachers spent a third of class time merely disciplining disruptive students, robbing her and others like her of valuable time necessary to understand the subjects and complete the assignments and tests. The teacher who has the training, respect and ability to control the classroom and teach effectively under these conditions is rare.

During the pandemic shutdown, the distance learning gave the above mentioned eighth grader the opportunity to study at her own pace, tune out disruptive students, communicate with serious like minded classmates and enjoy a successful learning experience. If she required additional help with a certain subject, even online, office hours to meet with the teacher were readily available on a weekly basis. From this remote learning experience she took away a few suggestions to be implemented when schools reopen. Make use of recorded video lessons after class to reinforce the classroom session. Offer or continue to offer, as the case may be, after school office hours weekly for one on one or at least very limited group meetings with the teacher. Compensate teachers for excellent classroom management and use these teachers to train those having difficulty with this ability so vital to effective teaching.[115]

Good points, but only a small part of the solution to this very big problem.

Classroom Discipline starts at home in early childhood and pre-K with the foundation for learning respect for authority, concern for others and care for property. Here is where we must instill a distaste for bullying, rudeness and other disruptive school behavior. But, as we have pointed out, critical learning experiences in early childhood and pre-K require the presence of a concerned parent or other in a parental role, typically the parent who works at home with time available for parenting, who works away from home but only part time, or who doesn't work at all. And this, as I have pointed out, requires a whole new culture guaranteeing a living income for families with children without both parents fully employed.

Assuming we can accomplish this, our children will enter their first classroom with a foundation of right and wrong when interacting with other children in an environment outside of their home.

Then the system for learning as we go through primary and secondary education should provide the appropriate disciplinary platform. Teachers who have been adequately trained, have the necessary skills, are well compensated, and are well respected in their communities will be successful. The system, however, should be capable of weeding out those who are not. That means that boards of education must be diligent in their negotiations with the unions regarding tenure and termination.

Of course there always will be the outliers, the student whose antisocial behavior cannot be controlled or the teacher who simply does not have the necessary disciplinary skills. If the principal determines that the student should be suspended or expelled, that must be the end of it, barring extremely extenuating circumstances, the superintendent, if there is one, should support him or her, and the board of education should not countermand the superintendent's decision.

But the final buck stops with the community. Based on the student's "connections" on one hand, or perhaps ethnicity on the other hand, disciplining him or her may be unpleasant or unpopular, but the community must support the board. There is no worse way to foster divisiveness, even hate, in a community than the sniping letter in the local newspaper written by a disgruntled parent or other adult with a bone to pick. Regardless, as we have illustrated, discipline should not be the same issue with online classes as with conventional in person classroom experience.

With these MOOCs as a model, online lessons in living courses can be developed by the governing body, the Department of Education or other, that can be taught at all levels of the formal education process, and even thereafter using other venues including The Great Courses method described earlier.

Coursera, partnering with 149 institutions worldwide, now has 24 million users taking 2000 courses online or at learning hubs created with the help of the U.S. State Department. The hubs, the latest evolution in MOOC thinking, are physical locations, where students including those who are among the 21 million people nationwide lacking access to broadband, or 157 million if we include those with slow or unreliable connection[116], can go to get internet access to free courses supplemented by weekly in-person class discussions with local teachers or facilitators. The learning hubs permit students and instructors to engage in personal discourse as part of the learning process. And the program includes non-paid Foreign Service officers and retired teachers as facilitators.[117]

And I see another substantial benefit from these alternate higher education opportunities. Liberal schools including the Ivy League and other prestigious colleges, are justifiably being criticized for the curbs they have put on freedom of expression, particularly of controversial ideas emanating from the conservative side. The result of this liberal "intolerance" is that students are too often being shielded from ideas that offend them, that hurt their sense of self-esteem, or that are contrary to the liberal core beliefs of the teaching institution. As discussed in Chapter Six, this protection has reached absurd levels, taking the form of "safe spaces," "trigger warnings," "microaggressions," and the stifling of guest speakers who might present ideas that offend them. Students, often without having even investigated what the speakers have to say, are allowed by college authorities to interrupt peaceful debates and shout down discussions. Like-minded faculty frequently lend their support to these often unruly protests. Higher education, by its very nature, has an obligation to offer open discussion of all issues, and to protect free speech, no matter how offensive to some students and faculty. Controversy and an open mind are the essence of a good education. While the institutions will be able to continue to censor some of their online courses, some of the wind will be taken out of the sails of students protesting the content.

Other Opportunities to Learn Life Skills and Lessons in Living aside from the Current Traditional Education Model of Pre-K, K through 8, High School, and College

I have contended that we can and should add our lessons to the already crowded curricula in primary and secondary education, replacing some of the traditional curricula if necessary. Looking at the lessons, as I have outlined them, civics and media literacy go to the top of the list for mandatory inclusion somewhere, civics, of course, already there in some states and school districts. But, throughout the formative years, indeed throughout life, there are a variety of other exciting opportunities for these lessons to be taught.

Weekly readers

Pamphlets in the order of 2 to 6 pages, if not already in use, would be an ideal teaching aid for those lessons that could be started in primary education for children as soon as they are comfortable with their reading capabilities and can comprehend the subject matter. They should include for the younger classes some of the very basic information in the civics and current affairs lessons. For the older classes, if and when weekly readers are used, the information would be more advanced and suitable for example for use at home facilitating discussion between students and their parents. The writers of these pamphlets would be either the authors of the courses or others selected in the same process described at the beginning of Chapter Six for the lessons in living.

Senior Corps Mentors
This would be an excellent pool from which to select teachers of our lessons when being reinforced in the required basic training term. These Senior Corps mentors would be selected based on their experience and expertise in the specific subject, and vetted to preclude political partisanship relative to any of the lessons vulnerable to this. Perhaps, for some of the courses, there would be two Senior Corps mentors, one promoting the more conservative position, the other promoting the more liberal.

Opportunities for Those who have Completed their Formal Education and Entered the Work Force to Absorb our Lessons in Living
Obviously there will be a transition period of a generation or more after this education revolution is adopted during which the youth will be enrolled in one form or another and many of their parents and other adults will be on the sidelines. They do not need to be left behind. All can get in the game.

The lessons could be made available individually on a menu similar to that now offered by The Great Courses which, in partnership with National Geographic, The Culinary Institute of America, the Smithsonian, HISTORY, and other sources, offers a "Journey of Lifelong Learning" including, as previously mentioned, 12,000 lectures in all academic disciplines, in CD, DVD, or streaming form accompanied by guidebook course reference manuals.[118]

Another approach might be similar to that of One Day University, which "brings stars of the academic world to cities across the country to give their most though-provoking talks." Typically, one or a small number of talks, or, when tailored to our subjects, perhaps one or two lessons are given in the one day allotted.[119]

Chapter Eight
Diversity and Compromise

"Try to see it my way, only time will tell if I am right or I am wrong."
The Beatles from "We Can Work it Out"

As David Brooks wrote in his column "The Strange Failure of the Educated Elite," when we address our fragmented society whose dividing barriers we wish to break down, we can think of the time when white male Christians, more typically Protestants, occupied the top rung. If on that rung, you went to a fancy prep school and Ivy or equivalent college, as did your father. You embarked on a prestigious career in law, medicine or business, climbed the professional or corporate ladder, and joined the best clubs. While, to some extent, this still exists, the trend has changed from a system based on birth to one based on talent. Institutions of higher learning opened up their doors to Jews, women and minorities creating a highly educated egalitarian socially conscious fragment committed to ending bigotry. But this was still a fragment. While talent had to a degree replaced birth as the favored aristocracy, now labeled as a meritocracy, inequality rose, the federal government became dysfunctional, and social trust declined. The educated meritocratic class passes its financial and social advantages on to their children creating an elite class further disassociated from the rest of society. The fallout is exacerbated by its focus on the individual who, from the time he or she graduates from college, is told to pursue their passion as they go forward on their individual journey. But, as Mr. Brooks says, "Life is not really an individual journey. Life is more like settling a sequence of villages. You help build a community at home, at work, in your town and then you go off and settle more villages." But the focus now is more on individual achievement rather than on building a society of harmony.[120]

By tearing the individual away at an early stage from its fragment and placing it in a living and working environment with individuals from other fragments, we can break down these barriers and help build the harmonious society that we desire.

How to Achieve the Diversity Element and Where Does it Take Us

When we talk about increasing the awareness and enlightenment of the electorate, of course news media, educational materials, seminars, conferences, courses, etc. all come into play. But arguably the best foundation to take advantage of all of this information is living with and talking to others of diverse racial, ethnic, religious, social and economic backgrounds. The required basic training term of national service participation would be the ideal setting, as it is now, for fostering the advantages of diversity for those enlisting in the military. But how can we accomplish something similar under a voluntary service program as now envisioned?

As mentioned earlier, in *Step Forward America!* I promoted a mandatory 2 years of service with military or civilian service options and a very comprehensive educational component including extensive civics study for all men and women when they graduate from high school, with options to defer until college graduation, and with existing programs such as the current military, AmeriCorps or the Peace Corps qualifying. But, while everyone is wildly enthusiastic about universal service, that enthusiasm quickly wains when they or their son or daughter are subject to conscription!

Based on all this, while I still believe that a 1 or 2 year term of service is the right course, and the only way that we will get those who need it most, those less privileged and left behind by society, to participate, I realize that this is not politically viable, and I now recommend a hybrid model consisting of 1 or 2 years of voluntary service preceded by a 12 week mandatory basic training. I think with enough effort by the elected officials and other influencers, this could be legislated.

During the last week or so of the basic training, representatives of AmeriCorps, the Peace Corps and other qualified service organizations would present, promote and encourage all in this captive audience to volunteer either then or later in one of their programs for the appropriate term of 1 to 2 years

We would develop a culture more like Switzerland's which includes 3 or 4 months of mandatory basic training, in their case mandatory for all males only, followed by diminishing periodic short training periods through later years. We would be accepting responsibility in return for our rights, but without excess burden to which the opponents of a mandatory program object—even this short mandatory training will be considered by some an excess burden considering that, when faced with the COVID-19 pandemic, arguably the nation's worst challenge since World war II, roughly one third of our citizens felt it too much of a burden to get vaccinated and/or even to wear masks!

How will this program work?

Phase 1 Mandatory Military style 12 week basic training: Realizing that 70 percent of our youth do not physically and/or mentally qualify for military service, this basic training will have different levels based on the participants' mental and physical capabilities. (Note that those bent on military service will bypass our program, enlist as before and go to the existing physically challenging boot camps.)

Training similar to Army basic training, albeit somewhat less physically rigorous would include
- tactical hiking,
- moderate obstacle course and rappelling,
- survival and first aid
- teamwork
- communications
- land navigating

- core values including respect, duty, honor, and integrity

Next. As part of the mandatory basic training are the refresher courses in the lessons in living detailed in Chapter 6. These are designed to support good citizenship as a step, in addition to a 1- or 2-year term in national service, on the road to becoming a good citizen pursuing and leading a productive life.

Then, at the end of this training, "recruiters" for both the military and AmeriCorps and other volunteer civilian service organizations, e.g., Teach for America, Habitat for Humanity and City year, would come to the camps and solicit enrollees for their programs from this captive audience. Without any obligation, they would promote the benefits to both the individuals and the nation to signing up then, or possibly committing then to serve after 2 or 4 years of college. We should expect this audience to be the main supply chain for our universal service program, certainly for those interested in national and public service, if not the military.

The New York Times columnist Tom Friedman during a visit to the Arab world and Afghanistan made a very timely comment attributing the power of our military to its pluralism. He cited the Air Force Chief who is of Eastern European descent, the woman Air Force Secretary who is a graduate of the Air Force Academy, her senior aide an African American woman, our base commander of Armenian descent, and his deputy of

Lebanese descent. Then too there was one of our servicemen in the control tower who came from Ukraine and a member of the combat briefing team whose dad was from Cuba and mother from Mexico. Mr. Friedman praised our military for combining all these people into one "fist" as he put it.[121]

Also, if the participant is part of a team working together on a civilian service project, such as many of the AmeriCorps assignments, we can expect results not too dissimilar from the military experience. On the other hand, many of the assignments in a service year(s) as now envisioned will not have this type of setting. Many assignments will undoubtedly involve working for a charity or a public service organization that may only need one, or at most very few, interns or helpers. Therefore, I would recommend that the federal department that certifies service in a particular charity or national or public service organization as qualifying for the service year certificate be required to provide a setting for this service that includes a working environment of diverse service participants and/or diverse regular employes.

Finally, I would argue that this exposure would be a significant factor in achieving our goal of maximizing voter participation in presidential and midterm elections, creating a passion for exercising the right to step up and have one's say in how we are governed. We would quickly learn that the "no one cares" excuse for not voting is not a valid one. We would quickly learn that the fragmentation and polarization that now exists, ascribing to the extreme positions of either party and turning to obstruction rather than compromise, are counterproductive to a functioning society. We can make laws and implement tax policies that encourage individual effort to get ahead while still building and maintaining a safety net for those who simply do not have the background, education or financial well being to survive with a reasonable standard of living.

Exposure to the opinions of others of diverse backgrounds leads to an understanding of, if not necessarily agreement with, these opinions, a consequent understanding of the positions taken by those running for and elected to government office, and a support for those willing to compromise.

From Tolerance to Compromise to Action

Now let's take a look at where we are now and where we might be. Remember that our goal is to create an informed educated electorate made up of a diversity of backgrounds, races, religions and ethnicities. This new generation will have developed a tolerance for different opinions and have the reasoning tools to examine a belief, a law, or regulation, existing or proposed, from more than one side. This doesn't come from listening only to the friends or elected officials who agree with us, by reading the editorials in only the publications that fit our political leanings, or by attending forums supported by only one side of the aisle. With so many issues being kicked down the road from one administration to the next, or perhaps even for decades, it is impossible to think that there is only one correct answer, one inherent truth, or one way forward.

Joseph Epstein in his *Wall Street Journal* article "The Tyranny of the 'Tolerant'" talks about avoiding the habits of those who, while priding themselves on their tolerance, their wokeness, their political correctness, and their progressiveness, when related to "sexual differences, minority mores, protest in all its forms," are totally intolerant of those who differ with them on issues where their own opinions are questioned. These typically include abortion, climate change, racism, and "government programs for the improvement of the human condition."[122]

We must be willing to say, "Yes, you have a point" when talking with people with whom we disagree.

In doing so, we can approach difficult subjects with an expectation of negotiating. Fortunately, there are many areas where both sides are in general agreement on what should be done, their spokespeople lacking only the will to take the sometimes painful steps to reach a resolution. In Chapter Nine, we list some of the areas where our leaders could make progress if they have the will to compromise. Suffice to say here, if, after trying to find common ground in the middle, we still fail to arrive at agreement, we will at least have shown good will. Everyone, however grudgingly, can then move on, their self-respect intact, more than ready to engage in the next challenge.

Citizens who Respect Others' Opinions can Support Compromise; Leaders who Respect Others' Opinions can Affect Compromise

The key to breaking through the dysfunction of our present government is to infuse our elected officials with a whole new culture of compromise. However, in a country famous for self-reliance, self-confidence, and independent thinking, a certain disdain for compromise has been with us since the days of our founding fathers. It surely reached a whole new level of intransigence however when then Senate Minority Leader Mitch McConnell proclaimed two years into President Obama's first term that the Republican Party's number one priority going forward was to restrict the newly elected president to a single term. Never mind accomplishing any of the urgent legislative priorities of the nation. Then, not too long after the 2016 elections, when the shoe was on the other foot, the overwhelming goal of many of the Democrats, then the party outside of the White House, was also to restrict the newly elected President, then Donald Trump, to a single term. As the fervor grew, eventually culminating in the impeachment, efforts by the Democrats for any meaningful legislation took a back seat.

Party politics is now the norm for everything. Vote the party line regardless of the merits. Issues have become so perfectly aligned with one party or the other that gridlock is the daily fare.

Larry Diamond in *Ill Winds,* his provocative description of the global assault on democracy, explains that the dread of compromise rather than strong political views is the real cause of the destructive polarization in our governing bodies. The fear is not bad policy outcomes, but rather that they will lose out in party primaries that draw the most committed and most ideological voters.[123]

But Mr. Diamond also finds some hope for overcoming this, discussing a bipartisan initiative, With Honor, "supporting military veterans of both parties who run for Congress pledging to embrace bipartisan problem solving and a civil tone over unrelenting partisanship." And he also cites other organizations, including No Labels and the Bipartisan Policy Center, with somewhat similar objectives.[124]

To be sure, throughout recent previous administrations, there were some positive signs that Congress started to realize that it must do a better job of compromising with their adversaries if they are to be effective. Take the example of former House Speaker Paul Ryan, addressing a bipartisan group of House interns, speaking about the effects that constant negativity bring to public perceptions of how their government works: "When people distrust politics, they come to distrust institutions. They lose faith in their government, and the future, too." Ryan went on to describe a better, idealized way that Congress could substitute compromise for hard line politics: "If someone has a bad idea, we tell them why our idea is better. We don't insult them into agreeing with us. We try to persuade them. We test their assumptions. And while we're at it, we test our own assumptions too." He admitted, "I'm certainly not going to stand here and tell you that I have always met this standard. There was a time when I would talk about a difference between 'makers' and 'takers' in our country, referring to people who accepted government benefits. But as I spent more time listening, and really learning the root causes of poverty, I realized I was wrong. 'Takers' wasn't how to refer to a single mom stuck in a poverty trap, just trying to take care of her family. Most people don't want to be dependent. And to label a whole group of Americans that way was wrong."[125]

OK, while we haven't seen much evidence of this attitude since Mr. Ryan uttered those words, that's the attitude we'd like expressed by all of our politicians. Now, imagine if you will, a generation or so from now, that we have all had the benefit of primary and secondary education that includes our recommended lessons in living. Imagine as well that many of our first generation of national service participants, those who had exposure to our lessons in living in school before their tour, have returned to their normal lives, either continuing toward college and university degrees or joining the civilian workforce in some capacity. Having had exposure to fellow service people or other colleagues of all ethnic, racial, social and economic backgrounds, this new generation of citizens will have developed greater tolerance for differences of opinion, a keen interest in current affairs, and will have their own ideas on what America's social, economic and political priorities should be. They will participate in government not only by going to the ballot box when called upon, but by keeping open communications with our elected officials, reading their newsletters, listening to their speeches, and giving them feedback on issues that they feel strongly about. "A good start," we may say.

Now imagine as well under this continuing scenario, many of us will have registered as independents. Whether we are independent, Republican or Democrat, we will abhor partisan obstructionism and will hold our elected officials accountable for their actions. Even imagine that the time has come to put an end to the long-running but inflexible two-party system, and that political decisions are being arrived at through the efforts of more fluid, shape-shifting coalitions. Inevitably, continued democratization and splintering within our parties will require a great degree of compromise from all involved.

Utopia? Dreaming? Perhaps, but if our institutions begin to change their current *modus operandi*, we will at least be moving in the right direction, providing a glimpse of what could be. And maybe, just maybe, we will step out of our collective shells and start working toward middle ground. There are, in truth, always areas of agreement to be uncovered in every dispute, always room to maneuver. Where can we start to develop meaningful answers resulting in meaningful legislation? It's easy to say that on most major issues there is no middle ground. But I disagree. If we step out of our collective shells, if we really listen to and read the words of those whose opinions diverge greatly from ours, we will find a middle ground. Let me offer some "for instances" on areas that we could and must find compromise, right now.

These, or the comparable controversies of the time, will be the basis of a final lesson in living The Art of Compromise.

Chapter Nine
The Art of Compromise

> *Every human benefit, every virtue
> and every prudent act is founded on
> compromise.*
>> Edmund Burke, *"On Conciliation with
>> America" 1775*

Here is our final lesson. Where are some significant opportunities for compromise that we can instill in our students and eventually our elected officials?

Gun Safety

Let's start with the gun control, better termed gun safety, debate. Gun control represents a classic case of the failure of our elected officials to compromise, legislate and govern. Whether we like it or not, the Supreme Court has repeatedly ruled in support of the Second Amendment that declares the individual's right to bear arms. This is not just an opinion capable of settling the matter for gun rights advocates. This is a fact for all of us. The Supreme Court, however, did not find that this right is unlimited.

Justice Antonin Scalia, writing for the majority in the District of Columbia vs. Heller case in 2008 regarding interpretation of the right to bear arms stated, "Nothing in our opinion should be taken to cast doubts on longstanding prohibitions on the possession of firearms by felons and the mentally ill, or laws forbidding the carrying of firearms in sensitive places such as schools and government buildings, or laws imposing conditions and qualifications on the commercial sale of firearms." Scalia continued, "Like most rights, the right secured by the Second Amendment is not unlimited." It is "not a right to keep and carry any weapon whatsoever in any manner whatsoever and for whatever purpose." In short, Scalia left us plenty of room to regulate gun use. So, regardless of where we stand on gun control, we must all admit that some sort of restrictions on the types and purposes of firearms are allowed—a starting point for further discussion.

Where do we start? Assault rifles? Most of us can't really even accurately define them. Regardless, automatic versions are already banned with some very limited grandfathering exceptions. Those in favor of banning semi-automatic versions ask why does anyone need these deadly weapons. Those in favor of allowing them on the other hand might make a somewhat understandable claim that they would give them an advantage over anyone breaking and entering and intending to do them or their family harm. While there is little scientific evidence to support this, it is an argument that gun control advocates cannot win.[126] Or the guns rights advocates might make another somewhat understandable claim that using semi-automatic assault rifles for target practice is a harmless, challenging and enjoyable sporting activity. Again, an argument hard to refute. And, there is no compelling evidence that the federal assault weapons ban in effect from 1994 until 2004 actually saved any lives.[127]

But, bottom line: Our rate of gun homicides per population is more than five times that of the next highest advanced Western nation.[128] But there is a middle ground where progress can be found right now if we look hard enough. It is found in two places, both supported by the vast majority of Americans, and they are **universal background checks** and **gun safety**. We are making great strides in many states toward enacting universal background checks; more than 30 states currently require almost all federal firearms transactions to be recorded with the authorities and go through the FBI's National Instant Criminal Background Check System (NICS), but there are exceptions. Federal law does not require background checks when guns are obtained through private sale or transfer, either inperson or through internet sales. According to a study in 2017, approximately 22 percent of sales fall into this category.[129]

Ongoing efforts in Washington to close this loophole have failed repeatedly, thanks in large parts to the lobbying of the National Rifle Association and their members. In January 2017, the new Trump administration had announced its intention to rescind an end-of-term Obama regulation that would prohibit the sale of guns to recipients identified as receiving disability assistance because of a disabling mental disorder and the inability to manage one's own personal affairs, claiming once again that it violates their Second Amendment rights.[130] Yet we can state with certainty that, were background checks applied to all gun sales, with no exceptions, the number of guns in the hands of those unfit to own them would surely be reduced, as would the incidence of violence and murders. Granted, many individuals with confirmed terrorist leanings as well as ordinary criminals would still manage to obtain guns from illegal sources, and there will always be threats of violence, but statistics from a study by the Center for American Progress show that gun deaths in states with weaker gun control laws, Alaska, Louisiana, and Mississippi for example, are higher than those of states with tougher laws, for example, Connecticut, Massachusetts, New Jersey and New York.[131]

The other place where consensus could be achieved is in "gun safety." Surely, everyone is in favor of "gun safety."

The term encompasses such devices as a childproof safety lock, a loading indicator that shows if there is ammunition in the chamber, and provisions for storing guns in locked cabinets when not in use. No, again! The NRA stands in the way of enacting gun safety measures, arguing that the mere availability of certain gun safety features slows access to firepower when it is needed in an emergency, and that such mandates are just another form of interference in gun owners' lives.

Deaths from guns in the United States, including suicides, homicides and accidents, now total more than

30,000 annually. During the past 30 years or so, there were more deaths from guns in the United States than in all of the wars since our founding.[132] Traditionally, when we see similar statistics surrounding other causes of death, automobile accidents, tobacco, unsafe food and drugs, swimming pools, children's toys and so on, we respond with appropriate policies and regulations to reduce incidences. By contrast, our response to gun safety issues has been limited at best, and now the likelihood of doing anything more is remote, due primarily to pressure from the NRA.

Following the tragic shootings at a rural Connecticut school in 2012, President Obama called on gun manufacturers to do more research into "smart guns"; these firearms use radio signals or fingerprint scanners to ensure that a weapon cannot be fired by anyone but its licensed owner, and thereby avoiding accidental discharges by children and other adults. The same technology also discourages gun theft, which when one considers that some half million guns are stolen each year[133] would surely reduce shootings significantly.

With these statistics, it's almost impossible to believe that there has been a long-standing ban on CDC gun violence research reaffirmed by Congress in December 2015.[134] The Dickey Amendment states that "None of the funds made available for injury prevention and control at the Centers for Disease Control and Prevention may be used to advocate or promote gun control." Contrast this with more than $2 million spent annually on traffic safety research! With no research funded for firearm injuries, we cannot know what works or might work to prevent them. We know that millions of lives are saved annually by research on the causes of traffic accidents and on cancer and other diseases caused by smoking and other unhealthy life styles.[135] Why can't we do this to enhance gun safety? Obviously, as mentioned above, lobbying by the gun industry and their mouthpiece the NRA, the totally unsubstantiated reasoning being that merely allowing safety features in guns would inevitably lead to mandating them.

Gun rights advocates tell us that features that are designed to prevent a gun from being fired by anyone but the owner are not totally effective and, therefore, should not be required. If that is the case, then it is certainly not unreasonable for someone to object to them being required. On the other hand, if they are at all effective, then no one should argue that it is unreasonable for someone, who has a pistol in his home and wishes to minimize the chance of it being misused by a child, to be able to purchase a gun with these features. Again, there is surely room for compromise here. With a little effort by elected officials willing to stand up and support the overwhelming majority of their constituents, this could be reversed.

Again, background checks and gun safety probably represent the most significant points of agreement that the majority of gun owners could accept. But there are undoubtedly other possible areas of compromise, for example microstamping of cartridges so they can be traced to the gun that fired them for use as evidence when investigating gun crimes.[136]

For more on this topic read *The Gun Debate—What Everyone Needs to Know* by Philip J. Cook and Kristin A. Goss.[137] The authors, both highly respected professors in Public Policy at Duke University, have thoroughly researched the history, advocacy and effectiveness of gun control and gun safety efforts here and abroad. There are no magic answers going forward, but if we look at the issues as a public health crisis, we can surely find a compromise that works for everyone. It doesn't have to be either the Constitution protected right to own guns, or the more basic right to life as in "Life, Liberty, and the Pursuit of Happiness," expressed in *The Declaration of Independence.* We can have both.

The Effect of International Trade on Jobs

Final agreements involve both the President and Congress, and here again opportunities for compromise abound, in this case between free traders and protectionists.

International trade has played an enormous role in global social and economic progress. Major milestones include the 1934 Trade Agreement Act, the 1947 General Agreement on Trade and Tariffs (GATT) and the establishment of the inter-governmental World Trade Organization (WTO) in 1995. U.S. annual trade volume now exceeds $4 trillion,[138] growing from 10 percent to 30 percent as a share of GDP during the past 50 years.[139] We and our global customers benefit from the technology and sophisticated high-value manufacturing and agricultural products and services that we create and export when the markets of the rest of the world are open to us. Conversely, we and our suppliers benefit from the lower cost commodities and less complex products that we import.

There is no doubt that trade agreements need provisions protecting workers from having their jobs exported to low-wage countries. But globalization is here to stay. Going back to an isolationist economy and building up barriers to free trade only involves the United States in trade wars, increasing the prices of goods imported from China, Mexico and other low-cost sources, and that would undoubtedly have a serious negative effect on the cost of living for everyone, but most particularly, our working class. It also will raise the cost of our production and thereby measurably reduce our export trade. And in the wake of preserving American jobs in industries where we do not necessarily excel, and where our products and services are not globally competitive, we ultimately will lose. Bear in mind that the jobs we are losing to lower wage competitors abroad represent a relatively small part of the manufacturing jobs being lost or that will be lost. More jobs are simply being replaced by robots, computers and other technological advances, and this will only increase over time. In the words of the American business consultant Warren Bennis, "The factory of the future will have only two employees, a man and a dog. The man will be there to feed the dog. The dog will be there to keep the man from touching the equipment."[140]

So, how do we counter these oft-expressed fears? First, make sure that in any trade agreement, including any renegotiated Comprehensive and Progressive Trans-Pacific Partnership (CPTPP), formerly known as the Trans-Pacific Partnership (TPP), or any new agreements with Britain and/or the European union, we are protected against foreign currency manipulation, intellectual property rights abuses, dumping, and other practices that would leave us at a disadvantage. Then enter into the agreements, but with the proviso that short-term trade assistance protection (wage insurance and taxpayer funded training as appropriate) is included for identified groups of workers subject to being replaced as the result of certain provisions of these negotiated trade agreements. That said, in the future, with improvements in our education system as addressed, we will hope that our work force is already better educated and trained for new jobs to replace jobs lost as the result of trade deals.

Regardless of any benefits of free-trade agreements, there are strategic security-related issues that should prevent us from outsourcing certain products and components in the supply train for them. For example, we must maintain the capacity to mine, manufacture, or otherwise produce basic drugs, drug ingredients and other pharmaceuticals vital to our health and safety, protective equipment such as masks and ventilators needed to combat pandemics, and precious metals vital to our advanced technology weapons. And we should maintain adequate strategic inventories of same.

Liberals and conservatives, pro-free traders and isolationists, surely can agree on these concepts and be able to compromise the details, so that new free trade agreements can go forward. Without a TPP or CPTPP, we are surely ceding power and prestige to the Chinese in the control of trade in the Pacific. And our position would seem to be further weakened by the Regional Comprehensive Economic Partnership (R.C.E.P.)signed in November 2020 by China and 14 other nations in the region including Australia, Japan and South Korea.

Welfare

Face it, we're all on welfare now! When we or our conservative legislators start talking about the free handouts that we're giving to the unemployed, or the vast numbers with low earnings who pay no income taxes, or when we complain about the amount of SNAP food stamps given out, we should look in the mirror. We all receive plenty of handouts: Medicare, for which the government picks up much of the tab; the mortgage deduction; the deductions for the taxes we pay to our municipal and state governments; the lowered capital gains tax rate that favors the rich; the avoidance of taxes on overseas profits; the "business expense" deductions that some people get for entertaining, fine dinners out, and travel; and a myriad of other tax benefits and loopholes.

The cost of food stamps given to those with low or no income pales in comparison, and we should all be aware that most of those receiving food stamps are not shiftless bums sitting around watching TV all day. Rather, they are hard working individuals whose wages simply do not cover the basic cost of living in today's America. These are not just the opinions of one side. They are indisputable facts affirmed by reputable economic studies. If we and our elected officials start from these givens, it should be a lot easier to compromise and develop appropriate safety net legislation. A renewed investigation and implementation of the role of "workfare," in which unemployed but able-bodied adults of sound mind are required to earn their public welfare benefit by performing public service jobs, would fit in nicely with a discussion of compromise.

Climate Control

While this has already been addressed in Chapter Six, it bears repeating here. Legislation relating to the effects on our economy and jobs of climate control measures is another area where there is some general agreement from which a compromise could be developed. I think there finally is no doubt in most people's minds that the climate is warming up, as even the Senate confirmed in January 2016, and that there will be some serious negative effects, but perhaps some positives too. Where there is still significant disagreement on how much of the warming is the result of man's involvement, aren't we at least partially to blame? We should continue studies to get a better handle on this, but, in the meantime, let's take a look at the steps that have been proposed to counter the effects of our alleged involvement. Would these steps have any benefits aside from reducing global warming? And the answer is a resounding yes. Reducing automotive emissions and reducing airborne pollutants from factories and fossil fuel power plants will have significant positive effects on health. And continuing to reduce the amount of oil that we import from the Middle East will give us more leverage in our dealings with our allies and adversaries there. Do these outweigh the negative effects of the alleged increased costs to the automotive industry, the loss of jobs in coal mining and oil drilling, and the costs of switching from coal and oil to solar and wind for generating electricity? I would say yes. Recent indications from the automotive industry are that the costs of increasing mileage standards are not going to be as detrimental as originally anticipated. There are opportunities for the creation of a huge number of new jobs in the solar and wind industries, far more than we will be losing in coal mining and oil drilling. Also, as mentioned in the above discussion of trade, we can develop a plan to provide wage support to displaced workers in the coal mines and oil fields. And, the costs of solar and wind power generation are being drastically reduced as we develop the technologies. In short, there is ample room for compromise considering the above positive effects on health and national security without ever addressing the role of humans in global warming.

And there is one other factor related to climate change on which all of us can agree. President Obama played the leading role in the Paris Climate Accord to mitigate greenhouse gas emissions signed by 194 member countries in the United Nations Framework Convention on Climate Change. President Trump by backing out of our commitment, regardless of the merits of the agreement, has caused our reputation as a world leader whose word can be relied on to suffer immensely. China would continue their leadership in the development of renewable energy sources, and we would indeed be looked upon as an also ran. Fortunately, President Biden has rejoined the Accord.

Job Creation

While the Republicans cry that jobs are created by providing favorable economic conditions such as reduced corporate taxes and the elimination of excessive regulations and laws, there is plenty of solid evidence that other approaches also work. Think back to the days of the land grants made to railroads to stimulate the opening of new territories and opportunities in the West; think of the Morrill Acts of 1862 and 1890 that financed the building of scores of public institutions of higher learning to educate the new generations of scientific farmers, scientists and engineers needed for industrializing America. Consider the direct government-created jobs in building new infrastructure in the 1930s, including the Tennessee Valley Authority that electrified a large rural area of the South, and the Hoover Dam. And who can forget the rapid and gargantuan build-up of the military-industrial complex beginning at the start of WWII and extending to the present. Think of the 1944 GI Bill (officially the Servicemen's Readjustment Act) that encouraged nearly 8 million veterans returning from World War II to obtain a college education qualifying them for productive rewarding employment. The interstate highway system, a signature project of President Eisenhower, and the Apollo space program that not only put a man on the moon but significantly enhanced our modern day computing capabilities are two more examples. The point is that we cannot discount the government's role in creating jobs. Deregulation to create a better economic climate for job creation is fine, but don't overlook the fact that deregulation also has its downside. In addition to reducing consumer and investor protection, deregulation can eliminate many office and clerical jobs that manage the regulations especially in health care, occupational safety, and environmental protection. I'm not taking either side now, just saying that the issue is not black and white.[141]

Healthcare

Under the Obama administration, the Republicans constantly wasted time proposing the repeal of the Affordable Care Act (ACA) when they had no chance of succeeding. Then, with control of the White House and both chambers of Congress in hand, the Trump administration in its effort to undo President Obama's signature achievement made a strategic miscalculation by proposing a totally inadequate "repeal and replace" bill. This time, however, the bill was defeated not solely by the opposition party, the Democrats, but also by opposing factions within the sponsoring party, the Republicans. This was surely the ultimate example of a failure to compromise leading to an inability to govern. Admittedly, in this case it was a good thing, as the bill proposed was a toxic mix of giveaways and takebacks that would accomplish the goals of neither party nor of their constituencies.

Over the preceding seven or eight years, the Republicans clearly had not done their homework. They could have picked some low-hanging fruit and claimed a quick victory by correcting one or two of the universally disliked features of the ACA. Then, at the same time, they could have done a better job of defining and confirming for comparison purposes the total cost of the ACA, the total cost of replacing it with an expansion of Medicare and Medicaid, the total cost of replacing it with a new "single payer" system, and the total cost of adding a public option. Only with that information, can we hope to find areas for compromise and the eventual development of something better than the ACA. One possibility that could get bipartisan support would be to stay with the ACA, tweak it to rid it of some of the shortcomings that the Republicans see, and add a public option as proposed by some Democrats and specifically by Joe Biden.

The Trump administration and the Republicans continued to promote repeal of the ACA, but as they neared the end of their term in office, they had yet to agree on and promote any replacement whatsoever.

Abortion

To be sure, in the long run, the resolution of the legalities and rights related to abortion will be determined by the Supreme Court. Accordingly, our say in the matter depends in part on us voting for and electing a President who will nominate Supreme Court justices sympathetic with our position, pro-life or pro-choice. The last three appointees would seem to lean in the direction of the former. But is this an issue that should be politicized and governed by the state, or is it strictly a religious issue? Doesn't it depend on how we individually define life or a person? If we consider the unborn fetus having reached a certain stage as a human life or a person, not a totally unreasonable definition, then it's hard to argue that taking this life is not a state issue. On the other hand, if we consider, for example, that a just conceived microscopic fetus is not a human life or a person, again not a totally unreasonable position, then it's hard to argue that this is a state issue and not just a religious issue. Wait, don't immediately make a judgment based on your pre-conceived notion. After all, this notion is more likely than not based on the way *you* were brought up. Ask yourself truly, are either of the two positions I have described positions that a reasonable, rationally thinking person, someone other than your family and friends who agree with you, would not possibly take? Let's look for other areas in which to compromise.

Neither side promotes abortion in principle. However, we can say that, in addition to a legal ban on abortions, with or without exceptions, there are other ways to reduce abortions. Planned Parenthood offers counseling to this end, which all parties can support. Planned Parenthood offers assistance with contraception that indisputably has a positive effect on reducing abortions. Efforts to defund and close down Planned Parenthood will only increase abortions. Perhaps there is room for compromise here.

Cuba

I am amazed that, over the many years since 1962 when we imposed a trade embargo on Cuba, with the exception of Mr. Khrushchev's failed attempt to install missiles, the Chinese and/or the Russians have not made more attempts to become more involved with the Cuban economy and society and gain a foothold in our backyard. The Monroe Doctrine here would seem rather "toothless" in these times. Since President Obama opened the door by using his executive authority to develop trade and travel, albeit limited, with Cuba, I think we should keep the China or Russia threat in mind, as we discuss and negotiate further with the Raul Castro regime. This concern could be the basis for compromise between those favoring, and those continuing to oppose, improved relations. Cuba's abysmal record on human rights will continue unless we seriously negotiate with them using for leverage improved relations to support their failed economy.

Raising Revenue to Fund New Programs

In the run up to the 2020 Democratic presidential primary, providing revenue for public investment to combat social and education inequality, and to advance universal healthcare, e.g. Medicare for all, was continuously at or near the top of the priorities list for which the candidates argued. One real sticking point at the time was a wealth tax. The moderates, Joe Biden et al., were adamant in their opposition, the progressives, Elizabeth Warren and Bernie Sanders, were highly in favor. The party, desperately looking to unseat Donald Trump, badly needed to build a platform of shared goals, but for all too long failed to concede that there were plenty of other ways to raise the revenues on which both sides could agree. The argument produced nothing significant in enhancing any candidate's favor and weakened the prospects for a united front against Mr. Trump. To build up the party's standing in preparation for the national elections, all the candidates should have been focusing on revenue raising means on which they could all pretty much agree, for example, raising corporate taxes, capital gains taxes and personal income taxes for the wealthy, adjusting deductions, strengthening the estate tax by taxing some or all of the gains on capital inherited by heirs, raising the limit for taxable social security benefits, and considering a financial transaction tax, all less controversial than a wealth tax which was unarguably a Constitutional and political mine field.[142]

Happily, by the time the party had selected Vice President Biden as its candidate, talk of a wealth tax subsided, and the extreme left and the moderates were able to come to something at least appearing as a compromised social and economic platform.

Move On! It Can be Done

In sum, there's plenty of room to bring our citizens and our legislators together if we are willing to seriously address both sides of the issues. We must start by listening thoughtfully and critically to the national news, preferably to newscasts that aim at objectivity and not to partisan cable news; it ends with communicating our wishes to our legislators and their doing our bidding. Avoid the temptation to push the "party line." If you're a dedicated small government conservative, understand the difference between an "expense" and an "investment." For example, increasing funding if it leads to much needed infrastructure repair can be a win rather than only a cost or expense. Don't let anger be the basis of judgment. The Republicans were so angry about President Obama's progressive agenda that they opposed some of the very same positions that they supported when the Republicans were in control a few years earlier. Unfortunately, during the Trump administration, the Democrats played the same anger game as are the Republican again in the beginning of the Biden administration.

Anger at Saudi Arabia for having harbored many of the terrorists who committed the attacks of 9/11 prompted a Republican Congress to enact The Justice Against Sponsors of Terrorism Act, which permitted American families who lost members in the attacks to sue Saudi rulers. Even when Obama vetoed the bill, saying that eliminating the historic notion of sovereign immunity would have the unintended consequence of jeopardizing

U.S. interests, putting American service members and elected officials at risk of being tried in foreign court, they overrode his veto and the bill stood. All very understandable, but the reciprocal has exposed us to lawsuits abroad for the many justified military and financial actions that we have taken that are considered by our enemies to be acts of terrorism.[143]

Perhaps President Obama best expressed the spirit of cooperation in his address to the 2016 graduates of Howard University: "If you think that the only way forward is to be as uncompromising as possible, you will feel good about yourself, you will enjoy a certain moral purity, but you're not going to get what you want, so don't try to shut folks out. Don't try to shut them down, no matter how much you might disagree with them."[144]

Let me close this chapter on a positive note. Congress can compromise. It can indeed be done. Back in December 2015, albeit almost three months late, Congress actually passed a budget without a government shutdown or the threat of another national debt default. The Democrats got much of what they wanted, i.e. no rider attached to defund Planned Parenthood, no blocking of the Administration's plan to require fiduciary duties of pension managers, and no undoing of President Obama's executive orders on immigration. The Republicans also got some concessions, i.e. postponement of the ACA's Cadillac tax on high-cost policies and the ACA medical device tax, legalization of the export of U.S. crude oil, the continuation of the ban on CDC gun violence studies, and enjoinment of the IRS from tampering with the tax exemption of 501(c)(4) organizations that perform as political action committees.[145]

An even better example of the ability to negotiate a compromise under challenging conditions is the Cares Act $2 trillion Phase 3 of the stimulus package passed by the Senate in response to the COVID-19 pandemic. With President Trump and Senate Majority Leader Mitch McConnell stepping aside, and Treasury Secretary Steven Mnuchin negotiating for the Republicans, the acrimony was at least adequately controlled and the massive stimulus package passed by the Senate 96-0. The Democrats didn't get as much as they hoped for, but they did get added funding for health care and unemployment and tougher oversight of the corporate bailout fund. Will the parties compromise on another major stimulus?

Perhaps the ultimate compromise we should be addressing in the aftermath of the 2020 elections relates to the bitter contest between the two major parties. Surely, there is nothing now that can define the Republican party other than the party of Trump, and not much that really defines the Democratic Party. That's a good thing. It would be nice if the 2024 elections would be contested by parties with completely new handles.

David Brooks in his *New York Times* article "New Life in The Center" envisioned a populist-nationalist party led by Trump, a progressive party led by Bernie Sanders and Elizabeth Warren, and a more traditional Democratic party best represented by Charles Schumer and Nancy Pelosi.[146] Tom Friedman wrote a column in the *Times* aptly titled "Dump G.O.P. For a Grand New Party" in which he described a center right party offering market-based solutions to some of the same issues that the Democrats address with their progressive solutions, i.e. climate change, gun laws, and free trade with protection for displaced workers.[147]

A fitting end to our lesson, The Art of the Compromise, would include a requirement to write a letter to one of our state or local elected officials either supporting or opposing their position on a current hot issue. For some, this will be a first, and, if so, it could very well lead to a lifetime practice.

Let's all do our part. With the teachings of our lessons and for some perhaps the experience of national service behind them, our youth will lead us in following the advice of the Dalai Lama, a world leader in promoting the benefits of bringing together people of different backgrounds. The Dalai Lama implores us to stop blaming the Congress and the parties and start addressing our own behavior to see what part, no matter how little, we can each play in making progress for our nation.[148]

David Leonhardt in his article "A Project To Nourish Your Soul," referring to the growing polarization of opinions on issues of national significance, picks up on the Dalai Lama's opinion in making a suggestion that we all go through a simple exercise. Pick an issue that you find complicated and about which you have some doubts regarding the legitimacy of your position, and grapple with it. Examine or re-examine the issues on both sides. Do some further research. Mr. Leonhardt, for his part chose three issues about which he had convictions, but admitted they were "tricky"—immigration, abortion and education—all three of which I have examined in the same light.[149]

We have discussed how any exposure, hopefully including a national service assignment, to the thoughts and opinions of others of diverse backgrounds enlightens us and makes us better more informed citizens able to better understand issues, find the grounds for agreement, and compromise for the good of society, thereby making us better able to select, encourage and support our elected officials.

Chapter Ten
Support for our Curriculum

> *What does education often do? It makes a straight cut ditch of a free, meandering brook.*
>
> Henry David Thoreau, journal
> circa November 1850

By now, I would hope that that most of you agree that an educational experience addressing at least some of our lessons and an exposure to the opinions of others from diverse backgrounds are critical to becoming a good citizen. As I have said, this could best be accomplished through a mandatory national service program, but that doesn't appear to be in the cards for the near future. However, it could also be supported by a mandatory basic training session added to voluntary national service as recommended by the National Commission on Military, National and Public Service. Many elected officials, widely acclaimed journalists, and other notables, past and present, have expressed their support for universal national service. And many of them have made post service educational benefits as well as the benefits derived from exposure to others with diverse backgrounds a key to their support.

William F. Buckley, in his 1990 book mentioned in Chapter Four *Gratitude—REFLECTIONS ON WHAT WE OWE TO OUR* COUNTRY,[150] made a compelling case for a one-year program of civilian service primarily for 18 year-olds that, while he described it as voluntary, becomes essentially mandatory considering the benefits that he said should accrue to participants and the penalties to be imposed on those who choose not to participate. He cited President Truman's advocacy for Universal Military Training that unfortunately never came to fruition, at least not in the framework that Truman had envisioned, and he also noted that even George Washington had been an advocate for universal service. Buckley used as a basis for some of the provisions of his program, Senator Sam Nunn's 1989 Citizenship and National Service Bill that offered, as a carrot to those volunteering, $10,000, in addition to ordinary living expenses, to be used for either college education or a down-payment on a mortgage.

Buckley examined all known models for a service program from a compulsory military draft to a complete voluntary system with no strings attached. His own "Buckley model" was to be administered by the individual states and overseen by a National Service Franchise Administration. While 18-year-olds were the principal target, older men and women would be welcome. A certificate of service would be provided on completion, and the individual states would determine how and when the year of service would be performed, continuous or staggered, and before, during or after college. The states would offer different service paths; for example in states such as Florida with an aging population, the focus might be more on care for and assistance to the elderly. In states with large inner city school systems, the focus might be more on helping out the teaching and administrative staff in these schools. The states would request and obtain approval from the National Service Franchise for all of their service functions, in order to set a basic national standard and qualify for a state certificate of service.

And here is where the carrot and the stick come in. Federal financial aid for education could be withheld from those without a certificate. Federal income taxes up to say $10,000 could be waived for those with a certificate. Colleges could be persuaded to withhold aid from those who were not graduates of national service. Those not headed for college who did not have a certificate could be subjected to other sanctions imposed by the individual state (Buckley suggested withholding drivers' licenses, but that seems rather draconian). A state that made completion of national service mandatory could then withhold a high school diploma from anyone not completing the program.[150]

Thomas Ricks, a fellow at the Center for a New American Security, expressed his views on national service in his *New York Times* article, "Let's Draft Our Kids." He states, "A revived draft, including both males and females, should include three options for new conscripts coming out of high school."[151]

The first option would be "18 months of military service with low pay but excellent post-service benefits, including free college tuition."[151] (I would offer some post service benefits, but certainly not free college tuition, as I do not equate all universal service with the opportunities provided by the GI Bill following military service in time of war.) The second option would be similar but substituting for military service a somewhat longer term of civilian service, and the third for those opting out would be no service and no benefits in return.[15]

James M. Stone is a prominent business leader and well-regarded economic thinker. In his best-selling 2016 book *5 Easy Theses—Commonsense Solutions to America's Greatest Economic Challenges*, he outlines what he calls simple solutions to America's most pressing public policy issues, from education to social and economic inequality. Discussing the challenges facing U.S. education, he claims that universal national service is the best cure. He agrees with all other proponents of national service that we owe a period of service in return for the privileges we receive from our American way of life. The benefits for the individual that he sees are exposure to the culture and opinions of others from all walks of life, and the opportunity for gaining technical training without the stigma of being put on a separate, socially unequal track from college bound students. Assuming the program is appropriately planned, there could be financial incentives for those going on to higher education, after the service is completed. Over and above these are the benefits to the nation that come from the multitude of services and talents provided by participants.

He proposes a one-year mandatory term to be served between the ages of 17 and 22, with an option for a second year. The participant would have the choice of serving in the military (probably requiring two years), in public works and infrastructure, or in social service.

Mr. Stone outlines other cures for our education problems, including improving the quality of high school education by adopting known "best practices" for curricula and teachers, but the best cure he sees lies in universal national service.[152]

Hillary Clinton took a somewhat different approach. Campaigning in Ft. Pierce, Florida, during the 2016 presidential campaign, she proposed a National Service Reserve to be called out in times of natural disasters and other emergencies, and to meet some of our ongoing social needs. Her goal was to enlist and train five million Americans, primarily ages 18 to 30. She, like others, noted that there is a large pool of willing volunteers and that only a small portion of them can be accommodated by existing volunteer programs like the Peace Corps and AmeriCorps.

While she did not go too deeply into specifics, she sees those administering the program working with industry to coordinate employed individuals' work schedules with their reserve duties, and working with higher education to provide course credits for reserve experience accrued by participating high school and college students.[153]

U.S. Representatives John B. Larson (CT 01) and John Lewis (GA 05) on July 14, 2016, introduced a bill, The ACTION for National Service Act, for a new national service plan with a goal of filling one million federal service positions with college student volunteers. These students would receive, as a reward for two years of service, compensation equal to twice the average in-state college tuition where their college is located, thereby addressing the current serious problem of student debt. The service opportunities would be in education, infrastructure, healthcare, disaster relief, and poverty.[154]

Columnist David Brooks who advocates for national service frequently in his writings in The *New York Times* is perhaps the most widely read supporter.

McChrystal's Take on National Service Arguably, the number one advocate for national service, is General Stanley McChrystal.

General McChrystal in his 2013 piece in the *Wall Street Journal* offered what was then considered a fresh approach. Rather than setting up a legally mandatory national service program, he suggested that we develop a socially incentivizing program, somewhat similar to Buckley's. In this scheme, colleges and universities would adjust their student enrollment policies and corporations their hiring practices, to benefit those who had served, effectively penalizing those who do not. In McChrystal's plan, 18-year-old men and women would be offered a choice of the five branches of the military, or several civilian service branches coordinated through AmeriCorps and other certified nonprofits, perhaps for one year, perhaps for two. Civilian service positions would be modestly paid (current AmeriCorps stipends up to $12,100 per annum are based on the federal poverty line in the region of service, plus a $5,500 scholarship bonus on completion to help with further studies). His original plan was endorsed by former **Secretaries of State Condi Rice and Madeleine Albright and former Secretary of Defense Robert Gates.**[155]

President Obama in July 2013 created a task force to expand national service "through partnerships to advance government priorities." In his memorandum, he stated that "Service has always been integral to the American identity. Our country was built on the belief that all of us, working together, can make this country a better place for all. That spirit remains as strong and integral to our identity today as at our country's founding. Since its creation 20 years ago, the Corporation for National and Community Service (CNCS) has been the federal agency charged with leading and expanding national service. The Edward M. Kennedy Serve America Act of 2009 (SAA) expanded CNCS's authority to create opportunities for more Americans to serve. This landmark, bipartisan legislation focuses national service on six areas: emergency and disaster service; economic opportunity; education; environmental stewardship; healthy futures; and veterans and military families....National service and volunteering can be effective solutions to national challenges....Americans are ready and willing to serve. Applications from Americans seeking to engage in national service programs far exceed the number of available positions. By creating new partnerships between agencies and CNCS that expand national service opportunities in areas aligned with agency missions, we can utilize the American spirit to improve lives and communities, expand economic and educational opportunities, enhance agencies' capacity to achieve their missions, efficiently use tax dollars, help individuals develop skills that will enable them to prepare for long-term careers, and build a pipeline to employment inside and outside the Federal Government."[156]

New York **Senator Kirsten Gillibrand** on the campaign trail for the 2020 Democratic Presidential candidate supported a national public service plan modeled after the GI Bill to give all Americans an education path to the middle class. Those serving one year would get two years of college paid for, those serving two years would get 4 years of college paid for. Those who don't want to attend a public college or who already have an undergraduate degree would get financial assistance for further education, to pay down existing education debt, for job training or to start a business or purchase a home.[157]

Former Democratic Maryland **Congressman John Delaney**, while on the 2020 Presidential campaign trail, proposed a similar plan, his offering two years of college tuition or vocational or technical training for those who had served one year and three years for those serving two years.[158]

One more of the many Democratic candidates supporting a national service program who tied it in with education tuition credit was South Bend, Indiana, **Mayor Pete Butegieg**.[159]

Senators Jack Reed, Chris Coons, and Richard Blumenthal also included education tuition credits in 2017 as part of their proposed America's Call to Improve Opportunities Now (ACTION) For National Service Act bill.[160] **Senator Coons** and a bipartisan group of colleagues followed in 2020 with their Cultivating Opportunity and Response to the Pandemic through Service (CORPS) Act promoting significant additional funding for AmeriCorps Vista, the Peace Corps, Senior Corps and like organizations in line with the recommendations of the National Commission on Military, National and Public Service.[161]

Former National Security Advisor **Susan Rice** in her memoir *Tough Love* spoke out in favor of a national service program that brings 18-to 21-year-olds in contact with others from different backgrounds and different locations to have to work together.[162]

In April 2021 **Senator Edward Markey** and **Representative Alexandria Ocasio-Cortez** introduced

The Civilian Climate Corps for Jobs and Justice Act of 2021 favored by **President Biden** and later included in his Build Back Better Act. This would mobilize 1.5 million Americans over 5 years to participate in national service in efforts aimed at controlling climate change.

Chapter Eleven
Bachelors of Citizenship

> *Indeed, we are strongest when the face of America isn't only a soldier carrying a gun but also a diplomat negotiating a peace, a Peace Corps volunteer bringing clean water to a village, or a relief worker stepping off a cargo plane as floodwaters rise.*
>
> *Colin Powell*

Continuing life enriched by our lessons in living, all it will take to be a good productive citizen will be, in the words of the environmental innovator Hal Harvey, to "Respect science, respect nature, respect each other."[163]

And assuming the efforts of "we the people" and our government achieve the goals that we have addressed and guarantee that we will all have an equal opportunity for employment leading to a standard of living that gives us adequate food, shelter, healthcare and education, and that truly encourages our pursuit of happiness, we can indeed be the great America that cares not only for its citizens, but for all the inhabitants of the planet and for the planet itself.

Where do we go from here? The National Commission on Military, National and Public Service should reconvene and add to their Report a recommendation for the mandatory basic training with its education component that we have addressed. Then a similar commission, probably under the Department of Education with input from the State Department should be formed to make recommendations for a universal upgrade to our primary, secondary and post secondary education as applicable that would encompass our "Lessons in Living" in a "Common Core for a Citizen Corps."

Those who have certificates attesting to their completion of the lessons in high school and/or in one of the other venues that we have addressed, have completed a year of voluntary military, national or public service as now envisioned by the National Commission, along with the mandatory basic training that we have described, and have also successfully completed one year of community college courses in a curriculum specifically designed for it would be awarded an **Associate's Degree in Citizenship**.

Those who meet the above criteria except with two years of service and two years of the above college courses would receive a **Bachelor's Degree in Citizenship**.

Isn't it about time that we reexamine our college undergraduate degrees. I believe that these degrees will substitute quite effectively for degrees in the arts and sciences in the job market of the future.

And finally, while any service and any education in civics and other lessons in living is part of good citizenship, there is a school that claims that citizenship will not be strengthened unless service is ingrained in politics, and this is a good point. Hopefully, many in the program will participate in public service leading them to life-long involvement in politics.

Kayla Drogosz, a senior research analyst at the Brookings Institution, said it best "Democracy functions well if everyone is, in a sense, a politician plodding through the muck of compromise and negotiation."[164]

Bibliography

1   Bernie Sanders, "Our Broken System, Laid Bare," The New York Times, April 20, 2020

2   Editorial, "The America We Need," The New York Times, April 19, 2020

3   David Brooks, "We Used to Build Things," The New York Times, October 13, 2017

4   David Epstein, "The Questions of a Lifetime," The Wall Street Journal, May 13-13, 2017

5   David Brooks, "Democracy Is a Way Of Life," The New York Times, January 16, 2018

6   Source unknown

7   National Commission on Military, National and Public Service, "Inspired to Serve," March 2020

8   Thomas L. Friedman and Michael Mandelbaum, *THAT USED TO BE US: HOW AMERICA FELL BEHIND IN THE WORLD IT INVENTED AND HOW WE CAN COME BACK* (New York: Picador/ Farrar, Straus and Giroux, 2011, 18-19

9   Ibid., 36-37

10   Ibid., 88

11   James Gustav Speth, *America the possible,* (New Haven: Yale University Press)105

12   Joe Nocera, "Reading, Math and Grit," The New York Times, September 8, 2012

13   Friedman and Mandelbaum, *THAT USED TO BE US,* 376

14   David Brooks, "This Is How Scandinavia Got Great," The New York Times, February 14, 2020

15   Christopher Brito, "Spring breakers say coronavirus pandemic won't stop them from partying," CBS News, March 19, 2020

16   Thomas L. Friedman, "Pass the Books. Hold the Oil," New York Times, March 11, 2012

17   David Brooks, "The Temptation of Hillary," New York Times, March 6, 2015

18   Jason Dean, "Weak Schools Said to Imperil Security," Wall Street Journal Mar. 21, 2012

19   Amanda Ripley, "What the U.S. Can Learn From Other Nations' Schools," New York Times, December 8, 2016

20   Eduardo Porter, "America's Students Are Lagging. Maybe It's Not the Schools.," New York Times, November 4, 2015

21   www.cfr.org/united-states/us-education-reform-national security/p27618

22   Claire Cain Miller, "Theme in Obama Farewell: Automation Can Divide Us," New York Times, January 16, 2017

23   Andrew M. Cuomo, "Fast-Food Workers Deserve a Pay Raise," New York Times, May 7, 2015

24   "How Washington, D.C. Schools Cheat their Students Twice," Wall Street Journal, December 1, 2012

25   Edward P. Lazear and Simon Janssen, "German Offers a Promising Jobs Model," Wall Street Journal," September 9, 2016

26   Jeffrey J. Selingo, "College Isn't Always the Answer," Wall Street Journal, May 27, 2016

27   Mark Schneider, "A Bachelor's Degree Isn't the Only Path to Good pay," Wall Street Journal, June 4, 2015

28   Sabrina Tavernise, "Another Casualty of the Virus: Americans' Faith in Washington," The New York Times, May 25, 2020

29   National Commission on Military, National and Public Service, "Inspired to Serve," March 2020

30   National Commission on Military, National and Public Service, "Inspired to Serve," Appendix A. March 2020

31   National Commission on Military, National and Public Service, "Inspired to Serve," March 2020

32   Elizabeth A. Harris, "One Lesson: Judge Judy Isn't on the Supreme Court," New York Times, November 10, 2016

33   Center for Civic Education, "We the People: The Citizen and the Constitution"

34   Eileen Fitzgerald, "We must have younger people civically engaged," The News Times Danbury, CT, October 10, 2013, A2

35   The Declaration of Independence

36   The Constitution of the Unites States of America

37   Bill of Rights

38   Amendments XIII, XV, and XIX to The Constitution of the United States of America

39   Larry Diamond, *Ill Winds*, New York: Penguin Press, 2019, 248

40   Timothy Egan, "The Dumbed Down Democracy," New York Times, August 27, 2016

41   David Brooks, "Why Sanders Will Probably Get the Nod," The New York Times, February 21, 2020

42   Michael R. Strain, *THE AMERICAN DREAM IS NOT DEAD*, Pennsylvania: Templeton Press, 2020, 32-51

43   "The Economy's Inequality Dividend," The Wall Street Journal, January 11-12, 2020

44   Paul Janesch, "How to evaluate a news provider," The News-Times, Danbury, CT, February 24, 2020

45   "Who Will Tell the Truth About the Press?" The New York Times, December 1, 2019

46   Alan Tonelson, "Following Up: Vital Background on 'Idea Laundering'—and Washington Corruption," January 29, 2018

47   Peter Boghossian, "'Idea laundering' in Academia," The Wall Street Journal, November 25, 2019

48   Tom Nichols, "How America Lost Faith in Expertise," Foreign Affairs March/April 2017, The Council on Foreign Relations

49   Coral Davenport, "White House Rejects New Emissions Rule Despite Covid-19 Links," The New York Times, April 15, 2020

50   MATTHEW ROSENBERG and MAGGIE HA-
     BERMAN, "More in G.O.P. Speak the Lan-
     guage of QAnon," The New York Times, August
     21, 2020

51   Daisuke Wakabayashi, Davey Alba and Marc Tra-
     cy, "Fake Theories Put the Blame On Bill Gates,"
     The New York Times, April 18, 2020

52   Annalee Newitz, "Nothing Lasts Forever," The
     New York Times, December 1, 2019

53   Barack Obama at a Democratic National Com-
     mittee fundraiser in Atherton, California April
     4, 2013

54   Greg Lukianoff And Adam Goldstein, "Law Alone
     Can't Protect Free Speech," The Wall Street Jour-
     nal, August 13, 2020

55   Michael Powell, "A Scholar Entangled in the Cul-
     tural Clash Over Free Speech and Race," The New
     York Times, July 16, 2020

56   Orrin Hatch, "Higher Ed and the Fragmenta-
     tion of America," The Wall Street Journal, July
     28, 2020

57   Yuval Noah Harari, *21 Lessons for the 21st Centu-
     ry*, New York: Spiegel & Grau, 2018, 200, 202

58   Ibid., 311

59   Matthew Hennessey, "My Daughter Is Driven to Learn Civics," The Wall Street Journal, March 11, 2020

60   George W. Bush and Karen Hughes, "A Charge to Keep" (Harper Collins, 1999) 240

61   http://abcnews.go.com/Politics/story?id=123290

62   George W. Bush State of the Union address Jan. 31, 2006

63   Dana Milbank, Washington Post Dec. 21, 2003

64   Jason Willick, "Does America Still Have a Common Creed?," The Wall Street Journal, November 30December 1, 2019

65   Noel Kashkari, "Immigration Is Practically a Free Lunch for America," The New York Times, January 19, 2018

66   Hal Harvey, "The Case for Climate Pragmatism," Foreign Affairs, The Council on Foreign Relations

67   "Nailing the Coffin on Climate Relief," The New York Times,

68   James A. Baker III, George P. Shultz, and Ted Halstead, "The Strategic Case for U.S. Climate Leadership," Foreign Affairs May/June 2020, The Council on Foreign Relations

69   *Drawdown*, New York: Penguin Books, 2017

70   Ibid., 98

71   Ibid., 93

72   Ibid., 170

73   Ibid., 53

74   Ibid., 45

75   Ibid., 39

76   Ibid., 143

77   Ibid., 89

78   Ibid., 159

79   Nina Sovich, "Econ 101 After recess," Wall Street Journal," March 2, 2016

80   Adam Smith, *Wealth of Nations*

81   Donald Marron, *30 Second Economics*, (Ivy Press, 2010) 136

82   Stephen Moore, "The Man who Saved Capitalism," Wall Street Journal, July 31, 2012

83   Marron, *30-Second Economics*, 17

84   Ibid., 51

85   Adam Smith, *Wealth of Nations*

86   Gene B. Sperling, "Economic Dignity for All". The New York Times, April 26, 2020

87   Andrew Ross Sorkin, "GREED IS GOOD EXCEPT WHEN IT'S BAD," The New York Times, September 13, 2020

88   Bruce Adams, "COVID-19 call to action: Let's make financial literacy a graduation requirement," The NewsTimes Danbury, CT, May 27, 2020

89   "The Center for Financial Literacy," http:/www.champlain.edu/centers-of-excellence/centerfor-financial-literacy

90   John Pelletier National Report Card on State Efforts to Improve Financial Literacy in High Schools, (Champlain College, 2013), 2

91   Stephanie Taylor Christensen, "Money 101: That's a course young Americans wish they'd taken in school," USA Today, October 6, 2016

92   Neal Gabler, "My Secret Shame," The Atlantic, May 2016

93   Friedman and Mandelbaum, *THAT USED TO BE US*, 301

94 Friedman and Mandelbaum, *THAT USED TO BE US*, 156-157

95 Ibid., 160

96 Ibid., 161

97 David Brooks, "The Golden Age of Bailing," The New York Times, July 7, 2017

98 Nicholas Kristof, "Will Our Grandchildren Scorn Us?," The New York Times, July 12, 2020

99 Yuval Noah Harari, *21 Lessons for the 21st Century*, 266

100 Ibid., 269

101 Paul Krugman, "This Land Of Denial And Death," The New York Times, March 11, 2020

102 Kim Brooks, "Forget Pancakes. Pay Women," The New York Times, March 10, 2020

103 Karen Cox, "Pre-K Curriculum," PreKinders.com

104 W. Steven Barnett, "Preschool Education and It's Lasting Effects: Research and Policy Implications," EpicPolicy.org

105   Courtney Schley, "INSPIRING APPS FOR HOME LESSONS," The New York Times, April 19, 2020

106   Alexandra Robbins, "Teachers Deserve More Respect," The New York Times, March 22, 2020

107   Josh Sanburn, "THE CASE FOR COMMUNITY COLLEGE," Time, June 12 2017

108   "Trump's Non-Celebrity Apprentices," The Wall Street Journal, June 19, 2017

109   Peter Q. Blair, "The Disparate Racial Impact of requiring a College Degree," The Wall Street Journal, June 29, 2020

110   Michael J. Sandel, "The Consequences Of the Diploma Divide," The New York Times, September 6, 2020

111   Thomas L. Friedman, "Come the Revolution," New York Times, May 16, 2012

112   Julie Jason, "Take learning online with MOOCs," The News-Times Danbury, CT, March 22, 2020

113   "Transforming Higher Ed?," The New York Times, April 24, 2020

114   Hans Taparia, "The Future of College Is Online," The New York Times, May 26, 2020

115   Veronique Mintz, "Learning Online Beats School," The New York Times, May 7, 2020

116   Kris Maher, "Online Classes Are Offline for Many," The Wall Street Journal. September 14, 2020

117   Catherine Cheney, "The road to real results for online learning in developing countries," devex.com. April 3, 2017

118   "The Great Courses," Chantilly, VA

119   "One Day University," New York, NY

120   David Brooks, "The Strange Failure of the Educated Elite," The New York Times, May 28, 2018

121   Thomas L. Friedman, "Charlottesville, ISIS and Us," The New York Times, August 16, 2019

122   Joseph Epstein, "The Tranny of the 'Tolerant'," The Wall Street Journal, October 10, 2020

123   Larry Diamond, *Ill Winds*, 263

124   Ibid., 305

125   House Speaker Paul Ryan, "The State of American Politics," http://www.speaker.gov/press-release/full-textspeaker-ryan, March 23, 2016

126   Stephan Lesher, "A Cacophony of Cowardice," Danbury News-Times, July 5, 2015

127   Philip J. Cook and Kristin A. Goss, *The Gun Debate*, (New York: Oxford University Press, 2014) 135

128   Kevin Quealy and Margot Sanger-Katz, "The U.S. Is a World Apart In Gun Death Rates," The New York Times, June 14, 2016

129   "Require Background Checks for All Gun Sales," March 15, 2018, Center for American Progress

130   Cook and Goss, *The Gun Debate*, 143

131   "Gun-Control Groups Push Growing Evidence That Laws Lead to Less Violence," New York Times, October 12, 2016

132   Cook and Goss, *The Gun Debate*, 34

133   Charles M. Blow, "Focus on Illegal Guns," New York Times, January 11, 2016

134   "The Republican Fear of Facts on Guns," New York Times, December 24, 2015

135   Charles M. Blow, "America Is the Gun," The New York Times, February 28, 2018

136   Nicholas Kristof, "We Can Act Before the Next Shooting," The New York Times, October 15, 2017

137   Cook and Goss, *The Gun Debate*

138   Frederick W. Smith, "How Trade Made America Great," Wall Street Journal, March 26-27, 2016

139   Jared Bernstein, "Free Trade Is Fading. Now What?" New York Times, March 14, 2016

140   Thomas L. Friedman, "At Lunch, Trump Give Critics Hope," New York Times, November 23, 2016

141   Eduardo Porter, "Government: The Real Job Creator," New York Times, May 11, 2016

142   Robert E. Rubin, "For Democrats, It's Divided We Fail," The New York Times, March 3, 2020

143   Curtis Bradley and Jack Goldsmith, "Don't Let Americans Sue Saudi America," New York Times, April 22, 2016

144   Frank Bruni, "Obama's Gorgeous Goodbye," New York Times, May 11, 2016

145 Alan S. Blinder, "A Glimpse of What Bipartisan Compromise Looks like". Wall Street Journal, December 31, 2015

146 David Brooks, "New Life in The Center," New York Times, November 29, 2016

147 Thomas L. Friedman, "Dump G.O.P. For a Grand New Party," New York Times, June 8, 2016

148 Arthur C. Brooks, "Bipartisanship Isn't for Wimps, After All," New York Times, April 30, 2016

149 David Leonhardt, "A Project To Nourish Your Soul," The New York Times, July 18, 2017

150 William F. Buckley, *Gratitude* (New York: Random House, 1990), xviii, 22, 116, 136

151 Thomas E. Ricks, "Let's Draft our Kids," New York Times, July 10, 2012

152 James M. Stone, *5 Easy Theses,* (New York: Houghton Mifflin Harcourt, 2016), 99, 123-132

153 "Hillary Clinton Announces New National Service Reserve, A New Way for Young Americans to Come Together and Serve Their Communities," https://www.hillaryclinton.com/briefing/update/2016/09/ 30

154   Congressman John B. Larson press release: "Larson, Lewis: 'Serve Your Country, Get Relief From Student Debt'" July 14, 2016

155   Michael Gerson, "National service can heal a divided nation," The Washington Post, June 24, 2013

156   President Barack Obama, "Presidential Memorandum— Expanding National Service," https://www.whitehouse.gov/the-press-office/2013/07/15

157   Kirsten Gillibrand, "My national public service plan would give all Americans a path to the middle class," June 2, 2020, FoxNews.com

158   Donald Judd, "Delaney proposes ambitious mandatory national service plan," July 28, 2019, CNN.com

159   Matthew Choi, "Pete Buttigieg suggests national service program," April 16, 2019, Politico.com

160   "Senators Call for ACTION to Expand Opportunities for National Service," November 2, 2017, Reed.Senate.gov

161   "Sens. Coons, Wicker, bipartisan group of colleagues unveil bill to expand national service dramatically in next COVID-19 relief package," June 16, 2020, Coons.Senate.gov

162 Emily Priborkin, "Susan Rice on the Value of Tough Love," September 24, 2019, American.edu

163 Thomas L. Friedman, "This Should Be Biden's Bumper Sticker," The New York Times, July 1, 2020

164 Kayla Drogosz, United We Serve "Citizenship without Politics? A Critique of Public Service", Washington, D.C.: Brookings Institution Press, 251

Made in the USA
Middletown, DE
31 December 2021

57351233R00146